# THE TRUTH ABOUT
# JESUS
## AND THE
## "LOST GOSPELS"

# DAVID MARSHALL

HARVEST HOUSE PUBLISHERS

EUGENE, OREGON

**THE TRUTH ABOUT JESUS AND THE "LOST GOSPELS"**
Copyright © 2007 by David Marshall
Published by Harvest House Publishers
Eugene, Oregon 97402
www.harvesthousepublishers.com

Library of Congress Cataloging-in-Publication Data
    Marshall, David, 1961-
    The truth about Jesus and the "Lost gospels" / David Marshall.
        p. cm.
    ISBN-13: 978-0-7369-2055-1 (pbk.)
    ISBN-10: 0-7369-2055-2
    1. Gnosticism—Controversial literature. 2. Apologetics. I. Title.
    BT1390.M36 2007
    299'.932—dc22

                                                                2006030662

**Printed in the United States of America**

        07 08 09 10 11 12 13 14 15 / VP-SK / 12 11 10 9 8 7 6 5 4 3 2 1

# CONTENTS

◈  ◈  ◈

# 1

# THE GNOSTIC
# RENAISSANCE

FOR 2000 YEARS, the world has tried to come to grips with Jesus of Nazareth. In the second century A.D., a king named Philip gave a bishop named Polycarp a choice: continue believing in Jesus and die, or "revile Christ, and I will let you go." Polycarp replied, "For eighty-six years I have been his servant, and he has done me no wrong, how then can I blaspheme my King who saved me?" Two centuries later, Constantine fought his brother-in-law by an old bridge over the Tiber River north of Rome under the sign of Christ's cross to become emperor himself.

Painters, poets, novelists, and composers who strode across the Western world like Titans found their inspiration in Jesus' life. Those who called themselves by his name invented the university, modern science, Gothic cathedrals, surgical procedures, and the Inquisition. Missionaries carried his words across the globe, inspiring reform in great civilizations and small Amazon tribes. Lights go up around the globe to mark his birth. Bells echo across mountain ranges to toll his resurrection, even in postcommunist countries, where the faith itself has come back from the dead. Millions of new converts pray to Jesus every year.

But do we have this Jesus all wrong? Long-lost "Gospels" now offer alternative stories about this man, and, some say, an alternative and better Christianity.

In 1945, near the town of Nag Hammadi on the bend of the Nile River in Upper Egypt, a farmer named Mohammed Ali unearthed a three-foot-tall red jar. He was afraid it might contain *jinn*, and hoped he would find gold. In fact, it held 12 papyrus books bound in leather. (And one more stuffed inside another.) These volumes, or *codices*, were written in an Egyptian language called Coptic, which used the letters of the Greek alphabet. Many claimed to have been written by Jesus' first disciples. Their authors were followers of an ancient movement called *Gnosticism*, from the Greek word *gnosis*, which means "knowledge."

In her 1979 book *The Gnostic Gospels*, historian Elaine Pagels introduced her many readers to the Jesus of these texts. This Jesus saved not by dying on a cross but through self-realization, like an Indian guru. Over the decades since, scholars and popular writers have used these and other lost Gospels to challenge the orthodox Christian story of who Jesus was, what he taught, and what his life means to us today.

The tale these texts tell is strange. The world, they say, was created by a demon (or "archon") named Yaltabaoth, identified as the God of the Old Testament. The universe exists through the union of beings called "aeons." "Archangels" tried to rape Eve. A sort of "body double" died in Jesus' place, while his spirit was untouched. Salvation consisted of finding unity with the "pleroma," a community of divine beings.

Forty-six different texts were found, varying in length, philosophy, state of preservation, and style. Some are just a few fragments; the longest comes to 43 pages in the Nag Hammadi Library translation (NHL). Many are the best-preserved or only copies we have of certain texts. Others have required painstaking reconstruction. (Mohammed Ali's mother used scraps to start a cooking fire.) Not all are Gnostic. Included is an excerpt from Plato's *Republic*, in which Socrates talks about "forms" and the "image of the lion." *The Sentences of Sextus* offers moral teachings a lot like those found in the biblical book of Proverbs. *The Teachings of Silvanus* was a best-selling book of popular philosophy, a kind of third-century *Chicken Soup for the Soul*. Nag Hammadi also contains a beautiful Christian allegory called *Acts of Peter and the Twelve Apostles*, in which Jesus appears as a pearl salesman and doctor, and commissions the disciples to "heal the bodies first…that you have power to heal the illnesses of the heart also" (NHL: 293-4).

But most of these works promote a distinctly Gnostic message. The story of creation is told many times, including in such key texts as *Tripartite Tractate* and the *Apocryphon* ("hidden teaching") *of John*. In several texts, the ascent of a Gnostic teacher to higher realms of reality, either in out-of-body experiences or after death, are described.

About two dozen Gnostic works claim to tell us something new about the life, death, or resurrection of Jesus. These are the lost Gospels that have stirred up so much fuss. Five Nag Hammadi works call themselves that: new Gospels of *Truth, Thomas, Philip, the Egyptians,* and *Mary*. Outside of the Nag Hammadi collection, the *Judas Gospel* and *Secret Gospel of Mark* tell pointedly subversive stories about Jesus and his first followers.

Some commentators think *earthshaking* is too mild an adjective for these discoveries, and expect aftershocks in heaven as well. Interest in these texts has spread from scholars to the general public. We once had to take the word of critical church fathers for what the Gnostics believed, we're told. Now we can read them for ourselves!

Famous scholars quickly made use of these documents to rewrite the story of Christianity. Many claimed the *Gospel of Thomas,* the most popular Gnostic text, told us more about "the real Jesus" than the Gospels in the Bible. Maybe Jesus was really a wandering sage a bit like a Greek cynic, and a bit like a Gnostic teacher, said some. Scholars belonging to a group called

The Jesus Seminar wrote a new translation of the "Five Gospels," with *Thomas* and the orthodox four. Some thought the *Gospel of Mary* should be added to the Bible not because it told the truth about Jesus, but because it made a woman the lead apostle. (And it rebuked Peter, generally seen as a stand-in for the orthodox church.)

But all this was like the pattering of raindrops before the gale breaks. The clouds burst with the publication of Dan Brown's *Da Vinci Code* in 2003. Fifty million readers have read that the Nag Hammadi writings are "unaltered Gospels"[1] that present a Jesus "in very human terms,"[2] unlike the Gospels in the Bible, which allegedly were chosen for political reasons. More than 80 Gospels were considered for the Christian canon, Brown claimed, mentioning *Philip* and *Mary* by name. Both soon appeared in paperback editions, along with dozens of other spin-offs. One version of *Mary* was edited by Karen King, who like Brown's fictional hero, Robert Langdon, is a professor at Harvard University. (As was Helmut Koester, whose views on *Thomas* helped feed scholarly interest. Koester was a student of the German theologian Rudolf Bultmann, who taught an earlier generation of pastors not to believe in miracles, and was also Elaine Pagels's teacher.) Bookshelves groaned under the weight of variant Gospels, histories of secret societies, books tracing the genetic heritage of Jesus, and exposés of Dan Brown's novel. Cover stories in major magazines, documentaries on PBS and the Discovery Channel, and Hollywood productions such as *The Matrix* and *The Da Vinci Code* have shown the Gnostic Rennaissance in full bloom.

Not everyone looks for the meaning of life in a novel or movie, of course. But the claims some scholars have made about these writings are almost as sensational, and the panache of scholarly credentials often fool the public into taking dubious theories seriously. The same year that *The Da Vinci Code* was published, Pagels came out with *Beyond Belief: The Secret Gospel of Thomas*. In it, she argued that the biblical Gospel of John was written to discredit

*Thomas.* She was greeted by large, enthusiastic audiences—I heard her speak to 700 people in a Methodist church in Seattle—as she promoted this theory. A young man who attended a similar meeting wrote, "I felt that Pagels was toppling the foundations of Christianity with her insightful discoveries." Other scholars with large popular audiences, while refraining from saying the Gnostic Gospels were historically accurate, used them in one way or another to render the old, old story of Jesus somehow beyond belief.

And so the lost Gospels are used to undermine Christianity in two ways.

For some, the Gnostic Jesus himself is attractive. This is not only true of readers who accept Dan Brown's theory that Jesus and Mary married and practiced sacred sex. (Which would have horrified historic Gnostics as much as it would Baptists!) Even before Nag Hammadi, the Gnostic picture of a world created by an errant demon found its way into the poetry of Romantics such as Blake and Yeats ("deliver us from the crime of death and birth"). Networks of Gnostic churches have cropped up. Followers of some Eastern sects also tell their story of Jesus in the light of these texts. Buddhists in Sri Lanka have made use of these works to argue that Jesus simply condensed Buddhist teachings.

Meanwhile, science creates its own fictions. It is in the light of a scholarly myth I call neo-Gnosticism that Pagels and her followers hope to reform (or destroy) Christianity. Scholars such as Pagels, Bart Ehrman, Marcus Borg, Karen King, John Crossan, and Marvin Meyer do not believe in a pleroma, but in pluralism: that Gnosticism and orthodox Christianity are just two of many valid ways to understand Jesus. The archon in Eden is the Christian church, which bids for power by picking four from off a tall stack of ancient Gospels and "suppressing" the rest. Ehrman suggests that the Roman Empire "might have converted to a different form of Christianity and the development of Western society and culture might have developed in ways that we cannot imagine."[3] The general assumption is that things could only have gone better.

If a tree falls in the forest and no one hears it, does it make a sound? It is not that no one has challenged the Gnostic or neo-Gnostic myths. Many of the most respected ancient historians in the world deny that these Gnostic writings shed any light on the historical Jesus at all. Others find the early Church less dark and devious than often depicted. But in the midst of the Gnostic Renaissance, these skeptical voices are swallowed like a few scattered leaves on the forest floor.

Who were the Gnostics? Do they tell the truth about Jesus? Can one find in Nag Hammadi, as eminent humanist Harold Bloom put it, a Jesus who is "unsponsored and free?"[4] Is the church guilty of a cover-up? Does discovery of the Nag Hammadi Library threaten Christianity? If it doesn't, is that only because Christians have their eyes shut to the facts?

Or do the Gnostic myths get things backwards, like compasses that point south? Could these discoveries actually show why orthodox Christianity is believable? Should a close look at the Gnostic Gospels remind us, by contrast, of the moral and intellectual riches of the Gospel of Jesus, which has flowed like a river for 2000 years, giving life to the world?

That is my view. In my opinion, the myth-makers have lost sight of the truth about Jesus, the lost Gospels (which are not Gospels at all) and of Christian history.

In the next chapter, I will describe the original Gnostic myth as found in Nag Hammadi and other writings. Not many people today believe this ancient worldview in the form I will describe it, nor is the telling of it likely to create faith. So hopefully the word *myth* will not seem presumptuous at this point. But in the following chapter, I will describe the growingly popular neo-Gnostic myth as told by Pagels and other scholars. I will argue not so much that their view of early Christianity is wrong, but rather that (like a myth) it barely tries to be right. Rather than seeking truth, Pagels and colleagues who follow her line distract our attention from truth with a sort of linguistic shell game. Three of the shells used in that game are the words *Politics, Gospel,* and *Christianity.*

I will argue that the Gnostics were not Christians. They did not write anything that can reasonably be called Gospels. The books they wrote are sensational and interesting at times, and have inspired enjoyable fiction. But a "Nag Hammadi universe"—a world in which Gnosticism won out in place of orthodoxy—would not be a kinder place. If Gnosticism had become the dominant form of Christianity, the world would be less free, women in particular. Love between men and women would be less cheerful. Gnosticism inspires science fiction, but would not have led us toward the benefits of science or taught this cranky world the love revealed by Christ.

The New Testament Gospels, I will argue, emerge from the challenge of the lost Gospels more credible than ever. They in fact are the source of freedom, fulfilling sexuality, science, and progress. And unlike the lost Gospels, they tell us the truth about Jesus and what he has done for our world.

2

# WHAT IS GNOSTICISM?

GNOSTICISM HAS BEEN DESCRIBED AS "Platonism run wild."[1] One of Plato's stories, written about four centuries before the time of Christ, is a good place to begin grappling with this complex and exotic view of life.

Suppose a group of slaves have been held underground in a cave since birth, Plato suggested. People and animals walk around and behind the slaves, but these poor souls are chained up so they can't look around and see them. But a fire behind the slaves projects shadows onto the rock wall in front of the slaves. All they see is shadows, and never the objects that cast them. Voices, too, echo in their ears indirectly, as if from the images. They tell stories to explain those shadows.

If a slave were freed so he could turn around, what would he see? At first the light of the fire would sting his eyes. But suppose an instructor were to explain his true situation? Reality would be hard to believe at first. If dragged, feet kicking in protest, up the steep trail to the opening of the cave and set free, the sun would temporarily blind him. The more substantive objects were, the harder it would be to see them. But when he finally did take in the outside world, all his old "shadow" theories would seem like nonsense.

But those still enslaved would laugh at the freed slave's stories of "Overworld." The suggestion that the experience of the person who had gone outside was richer and more real than their own might enrage them. (Plato remembered what happened to his master, Socrates, who was accused of corrupting the youth of Athens.)

Plato's allegory touches a chord with many who feel that this world is more than it appears. In the final episode of the classic *Chronicles of Narnia,* C.S. Lewis's heroes found themselves in a world that looked like their beloved land of Narnia. But the trees seemed more vivid, the mountains higher, and compared to the fruit, "the most melting pear was hard and woody, and the sweetest wild strawberry was sour." One character, an old professor, said it looked "more like the real thing." His friends looked at him doubtfully, and he added, "It's all in Plato, all in Plato."[2]

Most of Gnosticism can be found in Plato's parable of the cave.

Scholars debate whether Gnosticism first appeared before the time of Christ or after. At some point, Gnostics came into contact with Judaism and began to tell the story of creation and the fall of man to fit this story. In the beginning, they said, was "the Father," or "the One," beyond knowledge, with neither face nor form.

Contemporary mystics in India would have recognized the Gnostic picture of God. No one can see, understand, or touch him. He feels no desire, nor is he influenced by the desire of others. He is not "diminished" by need. He is superior to other divine beings precisely because he remains silent. He is not divine, blessed, or perfect—but something better. You can't call him either boundless or bounded, but some superior quality which we cannot know (NHL: 498).

The point is that the ultimate God is totally other, distant, and unknowable. He is "inconceivable by any thought, invisible by any thing, ineffable by any word, untouchable by any hand" (NHL: 62):

The form of the formless,

the body of the bodiless,

the face of the invisible,

the word of the unutterable,

the mind of the inconceivable.

God may be beyond experience or even praise, but he knows himself, and (perhaps) can reveal his nature. We conceive and speak words in an attempt to honor him somehow, but these names are just a trace of him. But the *Tripartite Tractate* does go on to give a positive, if indirect, description:

the fountain which flowed from him,

the root of those who are planted,

and the god of those who exist,

the light of those whom he illumines,

the love of those whom he loved...(NHL: 67).

Many Gnostic texts suggest that God is in all things, or that we can become part of God. The technical name for this is *pantheism*—"everything God." The most famous pantheist philosophy is found in the Hindu *Upanishads:*

He is the fire and the sun, and the moon and the stars. He is the air and the sea, and the Creator, Prajapati. He is this boy, he is that girl, he is this man, he is that woman, and he is this old man, too, tottering on his staff. His face is everywhere (*Shvetashvatara Upanishad:* IV, 2-3).

Similar images are scattered throughout the Gnostic writings.

Sometimes the awakened soul seems to merge with God. "Mirotheas, thou are my Mirotheos. I bless thee as God: I bless thy divinity" (*The Three Steles of Seth*) (NHL: 398). "Cast away from yourself blind thought, this bond of flesh which encircles you. And then you will reach Him-who-is. And you will no longer be James; rather you are the One-who-is" (*The [First] Apocalypse of James*) (NHL: 263). "I am the All, since I [exist in] everyone" (NHL: 513). "I dwell within all the Sovereignties and Powers and within the Angels and in every movement that exists in all matter" (*The Trimorphic Protennoia*) (NHL: 520).

Who are these "Sovereignties and Powers"? The answer involves a key concept in Gnostic thinking.

Up to 30 beings, called *aeons* (a word related to *eon* and *ever*) emanate from the Father. An aeon, like Mary Poppins, is a practically perfect being who dwells above. Aeons are male, female, of both genders, or neither. Collectively the "Totality" of aeons make up "Barbelo," or the "Pleroma," a nebulous realm of existence between the Spirit and the "low, ignorant, physical earth."[3]

In some mystical writings, it is hard to say whether there are many gods, or one God who calls himself by many names and manifests himself in many ways. The technical word for this is *henotheism*, and you find this concept in many Nag Hammadi texts. Each aeon is a name, a "power and property" of the Father, which are "intermingled and harmonious." One should picture these beings not like an amoeba splitting and separating, but like a single organism growing, "so that those who have come forth from him might become him as well" (NHL: 71). You could say, then, that the aeons are part of God, or are due to become part of God.

The writer of the text called *On the Origin of the World* was probably a henotheist. Qualities like Darkness and Wisdom pop into being. (The Gnostic myth is dreamlike and hard to pin down, which may be why the great psychologist Carl Jung, who wrote on the interpretation of dreams, found it fascinating, but Irenaeus, with equal fervor, called it "a stupefying blast of bombast.") Death mingles with himself and produces seven androgynous creatures, with male names such as Yao, Sabaoth, and Adonaios, and female names such as Jealousy, Wrath, Tears, Pain, Lust, and

Curse. Each pair joins and "begets" seven more (NHL: 177). God splits, and splits again, until a huge pantheon comes into being. Unlike most mythologies, no charming personal tales are told about these god-critters. They are abstract, inhuman, and poorly defined, like characters in the prologue of a play who disappear before the main characters step onto the stage.

The last of the aeons to come forth is Sophia, or Wisdom. It is her error that leads to the creation of everything else. (In some texts Logos, her male consort, or Epinnoia, her alter-ego, play the same role.)

Sophia should have created by union with Logos. But carried away by some feeling between love, lust, and curiosity, she desired to know the Father better, to "grasp his incomprehensibility" (NHL: 72). The Supreme God being ungraspable, she failed, and doubted. This doubt gave birth to a misbegotten "likeness" (NHL: 173). Evil thus entered the world through "self-doubt and division, forgetfulness and ignorance of (herself) and what is" (NHL: 73).

What came forth from Sophia was a "copy" of higher beings, the first archon, "imperfect and different" (NHL: 110). (*Archon* was the title given to the chief magistrate of Athens.) This ruler looked like a lion (NHL: 173), or "lion-serpent" (NHL: 110). His eyes flashed like lightning, and he had great authority. But like Plato's slaves, he was in the dark—unaware of his mother, the aeons, or the Father. Sophia hid this misbegotten creature from her aeonic colleagues, surrounding him with a luminous, translucent cloud. She called this Frankenstein *Yaltabaoth*. Gnostics also refer to him as Saklas, Samael, or the Demiurge.

They say he was the one Jews call Jehovah, Creator of heaven and earth.

## THE ORIGIN OF COSMIC CRUD

Yaltabaoth created more archons, and became their chief. With powers given him by Sophia, he created a copy universe and a variety of divine, demonic, and angelic beings to staff it. Seeing all he had made, he concluded, "I am a jealous God and there is no other God beside me." These words, which echo many Old Testament Bible passages, only proved (according to the *Apocryphon of John*) that the Hebrew God was not unique. Of whom was he jealous if there were no other gods?

Many Gnostic texts hold the central Jewish teaching of God's uniqueness up for vehement scorn. Several texts claim that when the Creator said, "There is none apart from me," a voice sounded from the aeonic world to chide him: "You are mistaken, Samael—that is, 'blind god'" (NHL: 175). *Hypostasis of the Archons* specifies that it was Zoe ("life," a female name in Greek) who said, "You are mistaken, Sakla!" (NHL: 168).

If the Creator, by whatever name, was a deluded fool, what does that make creation? In foul moods, anyone may feel (as Hamlet put it) that this "goodly frame, the earth" hardens into a "sterile promontory," and "this majestical roof fretted with golden fire" closes in to a "foul and pestilent congregation of vapors." But Gnostic distrust of nature went deeper than a mood. Nag Hammadi texts shout with protest at creation. The material world is a delusion, "dead creation" (NHL: 403), the "bond of flesh" (NHL: 263), "sinful flesh" (NHL: 276), "filthy mud" (NHL: 308), the "lowest region of all matter." Man is like a fish "bound in nets of flesh" (NHL: 475), dragged into the deepest muck.

Christians were a small, persecuted fellowship when these texts were written—roughly between A.D. 100–300—and the Roman Empire had decimated the Jews. Gnostics gleefully wrested biblical texts from orthodox hands to prove the vile character of the Creator, much like a guerilla band fighting with captured weapons. The Hebrew God forbade Adam from eating of the tree of knowledge, which means he wanted mankind to remain deluded. He asked, "Adam, where are you?" which implied his knowledge was limited. He cast Adam from the garden so he wouldn't eat of the tree of life and live forever. What kind of loving God would do that? The Gnostics anticipated the spirit, if not the arguments, of anti-Christian debunkers from Tom Paine to Bishop Spong and Richard Dawkins.

The vile character of the Jewish religion helped explain historical events. In A.D. 70, Roman legions defeated a spirited Jewish uprising, destroyed Jerusalem, and sent 100,000 Jews to Rome as slaves. (Two thousand died fighting wild beasts to celebrate the birthday of Titus's brother.) Fate revealed character. With Yaltabaoth as their chief, the Jewish capital had been a "dwelling place of a great number of archons" (NHL: 262).

How could anyone find in this convoluted, X-rated myth the cheery hedonism Dan Brown described in *The Da Vinci Code?* The Gnostics poetically explained why there is something rather than nothing, but in the process created one of the gloomiest pictures of nature ever conceived. Walk along the beach and look at a barnacled boulder with seaweed draped over it, observe a bumblebee docking at a thistle, or a sunset over a river lined with cottonwoods, and no one who loves the outdoors would need a Christian apologist to rally protest. Even Hamlet cheered up when he left his palace and sailed the salty seas for England.

Some modern Gnostics say their critique is not of nature, but of civilization. "We certainly don't hate the world or Nature, we hate any control system that tries to take away our ability to interact with the world independently," said one. "The aspects that are untouched by the control system are in fact divine."[4]

Maybe. Some Gnostics, such as the Manicheans, did develop the idea that fragments of the original spiritual light are diffused throughout all material objects. But it is hard to find a cheery view of nature in these texts. This sounds to me more like a form of what I will describe in the next chapter as neo-Gnosticism. Not only do the authors of the Nag Hammadi texts call nature an illusion, a trap, a tomb, and a "bond of forgetfulness," their silence about beauty is also revealing. The trees of these fields do not clap their hands. Sophia does not write poetry to celebrate the hippopotamus. The Gnostic Jesus ignores the lilies of the field.

## THE ORIGIN OF CASTE

Yaltabaoth was not entirely responsible for the creation of man. The Gnostic story is a bit like the nation of Islam myth of the mad scientist who created the yellow race from the dregs of black man, then whites from the dregs of the yellow. Both stories are complex because they serve the same apologetic purpose: to show that apparent similarities between human beings are false.

In *On the Origin of the World*, Sophia let fall a "droplet of light," which flowed into water. From that water she molded "Eve of Life"—"the first virgin, the one who without a husband bore her first offspring" (NHL: 180).

Seven "archangels" tried to rape Eve. This event is described many times in different ways. *The Apocryphon of John* says when the archons saw Adam talking with Eve, or her reflection in water, "they became enamored" and said, "Come, let us sow our seed in her." As they grabbed for her, she turned into a tree. The "female spiritual principle" then entered a snake, called (as in Plato's story) "the instructor." The archons raped or seduced the carnal Eve instead. She gave birth to "the last of the changeable bonds"—sin, injustice, blasphemy, forgetfulness, and ignorance (NHL: 121).

Yaltabaoth then created lower physical beings from which mortal men descend. In one text, the author interprets the words of Genesis, "Come, let us make man in our own image" literally to mean that man was made by a committee. Each part of the body—fingers on the right hand, left ribs, liver, veins, right thigh, left kidney, toes, toenails—was created by a different archon, 72 in all. Seven great archons oversaw the project. Twenty-nine commanded sensory and mental activity, four controlled the body's "thermostat"—heat, cold, wetness, and dryness—and four ruled the emotions. Altogether, 365 angels were involved in human manufacture (NHL: 115).

Another text describes human creation with less technology

and more drama. The archons "cast their sperm" into the earth to create a limp, spiritless Adam. Sophia gives him a soul and he stands up. The archons are infuriated. They seize and interrogate him, then lay him low again. Sophia sends Eve, who pities him and says, "Adam, become alive!" So while the mortal flesh was created by the Demiurge, spirit—for those who have it—has another and higher source (NHL: 182).

The same point is sometimes made by telling the story in yet another way. Yaltabaoth made man in the image of the archetypal man, Adamas, who, like the living creatures in Plato's story that project shadows, is the preexistent prototype or form of the mortal Adam. But when he breathed into Adam's mouth, unknown to him, the power of his mother, Sophia, breathing through him gave Adam a mode of life that Yaltabaoth himself could not experience. The archons were surprised and jealous to see that man's power, intelligence, and purity exceeded their own. So they threw him into the "lowest region of all matter." But (*Apocryphon of John* describes God as a couple) the Mother-Father sent Epinoia (Sophia's alter-ego) to the rescue. She "restored [Adam] to his fullness" and taught "the way of ascent." She hid in him so the archons couldn't catch her. They created a copy-man from earth, water, and fire and a copy spirituality and clothed him in a mortal body, his "tomb" and "bond of forgetfulness" (NHL: 105-23).

Most Gnostics believed there were three kinds of people: spiritual, psychic, and material. The nature of each person was revealed by how he responded to the Gnostic message. The spiritual believed immediately. The psychic (orthodox Christians) responded more slowly, while the material shunned "the shining of the light" and directed "hatred and envy and jealousy" toward the church (NHL: 96). The fate of each soul parallels its nature: ascent to the Father, ascent to a lower level of salvation (what Joseph Smith, who had a similar idea, called the *terrestrial kingdom*), or destruction.

If what you were determined your fate, why did the Gnostic message need to be preached?

This story, too, was told in different ways. The chief archon made all humanity drink the "water of forgetfulness," said the *Apocryphon of John,* so that like Plato's slaves, we do not know where we are from (NHL: 119). In *On the Origin of the World,* seven rulers contest with "the instructor," the serpent. After Adam and Eve name the animals, the archons worry that Adam "has come to be like one of us, so that he knows the difference between the light and the darkness." They expel the couple, and their lives are shortened. Sophia Zoe becomes indignant that mankind has been cursed, and casts the archons out of heaven to become evil spirits on the earth. The fiery phoenix kills itself as a witness against them (NHL: 186).

The chief archon plans a flood to destroy the evidence—awareness of our true nature. Many people (along with Noah) hide from the floodwaters. The world grows dark. Emerging from the ark, Noah tells his sons to serve the chief archon "in fear and slavery all the days of your lives" (NHL: 281).

## GNOSIS, THE PATH TO HEAVEN

Gnostics did not believe that salvation came as a gift from God the Creator, since he was jealous and did not want us saved. Nor could it come directly from the Father, who does not act in this world. Nor could it come by trust in a Savior who died on the cross. Most Gnostics denied that Jesus died, as we will see later.

Nor, again, did salvation come through good works. Harvard historian Karen King claimed to find in the *Gospel of Mary* "an ethical orientation toward conformity with the pattern of the Good."[5] This claim is often repeated by fans of the Gnostic scriptures, but there is little evidence for it. In all the Nag Hammadi literature, the silence on the subjects of kindness and right and wrong is deafening, as we will see.

Salvation, then, does not come by faith or works, or from God or because of anything Jesus has done. Nor can it come at all for most of humanity. How can the spiritual escape this world? Through *gnosis*.

*Gnosis* is Greek for "knowledge." *Gnosticism* can be defined simply as "salvation by knowledge." The sort of knowledge Gnostics sought was not science, technology, or education, which would involve manipulating the shadow world to create gross material wealth. Knowledge of the self was the key to liberation.

To this point, the Gnostic myth follows Plato's parable of the cave closely. We are slaves in an unreal world. Evil masters keep us "below," "in the dark," in "nets of flesh." But beyond and above lies the real world, to which we may hope to ascend. Gnostics also agree with the dictum written in gold over the temple to Apollo, "Know Yourself," which meant for them, as for Hindus, "realize your true nature."

The Gnostics also followed Plato in seeing worldly objects as shadows of higher forms. The worlds were copies of aeons. Eve was a copy of Divine Wisdom, through whose error the world came into being. The mortal Jesus was a copy of Adamas, and died on the cross in his place. Animals correspond to eternal master copies. Even terrestrial trees were images of immortal ones bearing "imperishable fruit" (NHL: 416).

After death, one could ascend from lower, hellish realms to the true heavens. One "stripped" oneself of the body in order to "clothe" oneself, casting away the "bond of flesh" (NHL: 263). Redemption meant release from the power of the controllers and "ascent" to the Pleroma, to peace and light.

What we needed was an instructor.

Gnostics identified the instructor with the snake in the garden of Eden. He also came in the person of Jesus and in other forms.

In the *Apocalypse of Paul*, Paul met a child who greeted Paul by saying, "I know who you are." This child, an appearance of Jesus, guided Paul through a series of seven heavens (though hell or purgatory capture their character more closely). Paul saw angels whipping sinners. He encountered a toll collector whose job seemed to be keeping souls from ascending too high without proper authorization. In the seventh heaven, Paul met an old man who asked where he wanted to go. "I am going to the place from which I came…down to the world of the dead in order to lead captive the captivity that was led in the captivity of Babylon," Paul responded, giving the correct answer (NHL: 257-9). Answering such questions correctly after death was the key to ascending to higher levels.

What role did Jesus play in the Gnostic system? In *On the Origin of the World,* Faith rebukes Yaltabaoth for calling himself the one true God. She then prophesies that an "immortal man of light" who existed before him would appear "among your modeled forms" and "trample you to scorn" (NHL: 175). Jesus was that man.

Jesus served Gnostics, then, both as a guide and a teacher (more on this later). Because he was eternal and from above, we, too, can be restored to the Pleroma. Confessing Christ, we can escape the "multiplicity of forms," "inequality," and "change." In the beginning, all was One, and that is the aim, too: unity not only in love (as Paul said) but in essence, "where there is no male nor female, nor slave and free, nor circumcision and uncircumcision, *neither angel nor man,* but Christ is all in all" (*Tripartite Tractate,* NHL: 101). After "the true man" explains things, those saved will no longer be deceived by matter. They will trample death under foot and ascend into "limitless light." Jesus will "receive" the "Christ," Sophia will rejoin the Pleroma, and "the All will come to be in unity and reconciliation" (NHL: 487).

Scholars will remind you again that there were many Gnostic schools. Gnosticism was suppressed by the church and died out in the West. It reappeared to influence the Cathari in medieval France, and the Romantics several centuries later. But Gnosticism would enjoy a long career in the East. A third-century Gnostic teacher called Mani started a syncretistic religion called Man-ichaeism, which spread through central Asia and as far as China. It influenced the Mongol court, and some say the name of the Ming Dynasty (*Ming* means "light") shows Manichean influence.

Read a few Gnostic texts and get a taste on the tongue. It is not hard to recognize that flavor again, whether you meet it in books, movies, or poetry—the dreamlike sense that time, place, and personality are moving in and out of one another, the distant Supreme God, emanations, a female aeon and her creative misadventures, hatred of the Creator, and the salvation that comes when you "know who you are," as *Lion King* puts it.

But the most popular modern form of the Gnostic myth is what I call neo-Gnosticism. This faith is especially popular with scholars who cannot believe in classical Gnosticism, yet who still hate the Christian God and want to destroy faith in him.

3

# GNOSTICISM REBOOTED

IN THE CHILDREN'S story *The Last Battle*, a treacherous ape, in league with foreign enemies, dressed a donkey in a lion's skin to fool the animal residents of the land of Narnia into thinking he was Aslan, the true king of the beasts. Loyalists captured the donkey, liberated a group of dwarves who were being marched to the salt mines, and showed them the captive, bedraggled lion skin still draped over him. Rather than being grateful and joining the fight for freedom, the dwarf Griffle responded with skepticism when he was told that the donkey was merely an imitation of the real Aslan. "And you've got a better imitation, I suppose!" said Griffle. "No thanks. We've been fooled once and we're not going to be fooled again. The dwarfs are for the dwarfs!"[1]

The problem with lies is not only that some people believe them, but that they degrade the concept of truth. Historian Edward Gibbon said that in ancient Rome, philosophers saw all religions as equally false, commoners saw them as equally true, and magistrates found them equally useful. Maybe the sages became exasperated because ordinary folk didn't care about truth. Or maybe the folk grasped at straws because they saw that the sages had become too cynical to care. And how can you prove religious claims, anyway? If you see a lion far off by moonlight, how do you know it's real? Whose interests are furthered by the "orthodox Aslan"? Jesus lived 2000 years ago, and we only know about him from people whom we've never met. How do we know the story isn't just some sneaky trick?

Some scholars use the Gnostic texts to tell an influential story of Christianity that plays to such concerns and creates what I call the neo-Gnostic myth. Elaine Pagels's *The Gnostic Gospels* gives the classic version of the story, which is concise, eloquent, and highly influential. Every theme Pagels introduced in her 1979 book has been repeated by other well-known scholars and popular writers. Major media sources often tell the story of the Gnostic Gospels as if they were paraphrasing Pagels—and often they are, when they don't quote her directly.

I call this myth neo-Gnostic because, like the Gnostic tale from which it comes, it tells of Paradise Lost through ignorance and political maneuvering, and offers the hope that some special knowledge, contained in books about Jesus, will unlatch the gate to freedom.

To most people, *myth* means "untrue story." Anthropologists use the word to describe "a tale, often about origins, told to explain why things are as they are."[2] Neo-Gnosticism is a myth in both senses. It tells a story about the origin of Christianity that seeks to explain what went wrong in Western history: why Christians believe in the resurrection of Christ, and why the West held inquisitions, launched crusades, mistreated women, and burned witches. Also, while this neo-Gnostic myth contains factual elements and raises some serious questions, on every important point it is deeply mistaken—as I will show in the pages to come.

## THE NEO-GNOSTIC MYTH

Those who first told this story are scholars who play by the "official unofficial" academic rule book. Rule number one in that book is "methodological naturalism"—in other words, no appeals to divine intervention to explain phenomena. The neo-Gnostic creation myth therefore begins with man, not God: the "historical Jesus" from whom the Christian church emerged, whether intentionally or (many argue) by accident. In feminist versions of the myth, Mary Magdalene plays an almost equally prominent role, giving the church a "father-mother" creator as found in some forms of Gnosticism.

Gnostics say God is unknowable, but he is more good than our ordinary concepts of virtue can express. Neo-Gnosticism has its roots in a radical scholarship that sees Jesus a similar way. On the one hand, they claim, the Gospels are too late, too contradictory, or too biased to yield a reliable picture of the real Jesus. The Gospels need to be interrogated, filtered, and sifted to separate truth from sanctified lies. Most agree that the character and teaching of Jesus transcended conventional ideas about virtue that dominated Jewish and Greco-Roman cultures. Jesus seemed amazingly free of the social and caste prejudices by which people of his time tried to approximate purity and holiness. He ate with priests and economic pillars of society as well as prostitutes and Roman syncophants. He helped the weak and oppressed. It is also clear that Jesus was brilliant. No ordinary pundit or church hack could have invented his parables. The Gospels are also full of witty aphorisms, one-liners that crystallize truth and still whack us on the head and make us think.

About A.D. 30, Jesus was killed by the Roman governor Pontius Pilate. What happened next? There are different stories, says Pagels, and we can't know which is right.

What we do know is that a few years later, a rabbi named Saul had a vision of Jesus while traveling to Syria. He came to believe Jesus was the Messiah, sent to save not only the Jews but all humanity. As Saul, now called Paul, preached his message about reconciliation to God through Jesus around the Mediterranean world, it was welcomed partly because the new faith was more inclusive than earlier forms of Judaism. Hebrew converts had been required to follow Jewish customs, including the never-popular rite of circumcision. But though Paul was a Jew, he told other peoples that they could join the "spiritual Israel" without adhering to this ancient and painful Hebrew custom.

Here we must be careful not to commit the sin of anachronism, we are warned: reading later conditions into earlier events. Soon the Mediterranean world was abuzz not with a Gospel approved by some rigid, hierarchical church, with its limited collection of approved books and strictly defined beliefs, but a disparate grab bag of teachings "far more diverse than orthodox sources chose to indicate," as Pagels put it.[3]

Herbert Krosney claims that in the early days, there were "thirty or more" Gospels, "all proclaiming that they were the truth."[4] If so, Gospels in the new Gnostic myth correspond in number to aeons in the old. The point in both cases is that divine truth is not a monopoly. God comes in different forms and is summoned by different names. Since neo-Gnostics often understand religion in psychological or aesthetic terms, they see each interpretation as equally legitimate. Religion borrows its shape from society, and may in turn shape society. Letting everyone bring his own Gospel to the table seems more democratic than approving some and banning others, which early Christians are said to have done.

Orthodox Christianity, or "proto-orthodoxy" as Karen King calls it, was but one of many Christianities that appeared around the ancient Mediterranean world.

Among the early sects were followers of Marcion, who denied that a single God was responsible for both testaments of the Bible. Marcion believed Jesus came to save mankind from the vengeful God of the Jews. Jesus could not have been part of a universe created by that God. He only appeared to be human and to suffer. Gnostics adopted this view of Jesus, called *Docetism*.

Several schools of Gnostics were among the diverse communities that professed to follow Jesus: students of Carpocrates,

Saturninus, Basilides, Cerdo, Apelles, Valentinus, and Mani. The second-century cities in which these teachings took root were lively, multicultural enclaves, with people of many tribes and languages mixing wares and gods under the peace of Rome. Old traditions were challenged and molded by Greek philosophy and saga, Babylonian magic, Egyptian gods, Indian mysticism, and Jewish religious history. The religions of the world were spread out as if for a vast banquet. Gnosticism was just one—or several, rather—of many new innovative and tantalizing spiritual cuisines.

Neo-Gnostics also find the idea of salvation through knowledge attractive. A Gnostic was a disciple of his own mind. Pagels claimed that modern psychology has proven that "the psyche bears within itself the potential for liberation or destruction."[5] Carl Jung, one of the world's most influential psychologists, purchased a Nag Hammadi codex, now called the "Jung codex," and often referred to Gnostic ideas. One thing Jung liked was the Gnostic idea that the psyche can and must save itself. (Though Pagels is mistaken if she thinks all psychologists agree![6]) Jung was also fascinated by the dreamlike nature of many Gnostic writings, finding in them (as in dreams) suggestive psychological symbols. (He often mentions Gnosticism in *Psychology and Religion*, for example.)

## YALTABAOTH IS BORN

Pagels claimed there is a "range of interpretations" of the resurrection even in the New Testament.[7] Paul, she argued, did not seem to meet the risen Christ the same way as Mary or Peter met him. Maybe Paul simply experienced a vision brought on by stress. In later centuries, Christian leaders would insist that only the literal interpretation of the resurrection was acceptable. This gave them special authority. To say, "I have seen the risen Christ," meant, "I am an apostle called by God." In other words, "If you want your soul saved, you must listen to me."

Peter claimed he saw Jesus alive. As a result, "shortly after

Jesus' death, Peter took charge of the group as its leader and spokesman."[8] Pagels is a little inconsistent here: She admits that actually Mary Magdalene was first to see Jesus. Tucker Malarkey, in her novel on the discovery of the Nag Hammadi writings, *Resurrection* (in the notes to which she describes herself as "incredibly grateful" that Elaine Pagels "is on the earth, building such crucial bridges of understanding"), smoothes the discrepancy over by claiming that Mary only claimed to see Jesus in a spiritual vision, rather than in the flesh.[9] In any case, the authority of the "small band" who saw the living Jesus became "incontestable."[10] John told stories of Jesus to the young Polycarp, who later became the leader of the church in the important port city of Smyrna. Ecclesiastic bureaucracy self-organized like molecules lining up in a crystal. The chain of testimony was used to establish a hierarchy of offices, an apostolic succession passed from bishop to bishop, culminating in the Catholic pope.

Even non-Christians often find the story of the early church romantic, like the account of David's defeat of Goliath. Historian Will Durant wrote,

> There is no greater drama in human record than the sight of a few Christians, scorned or oppressed by a succession of emperors, bearing all trials with a fierce tenacity, multiplying quietly, building order while their enemies generated chaos, fighting the sword with the word, brutality with hope, and at last defeating the strongest state that history had known. Caesar and Christ had met in the arena, and Christ had won.[11]

The problem with David, from the postmodern perspective that neo-Gnostic scholars often hold, is that after he cut off Goliath's head, he took his sword and became king himself.

Neither was Caesar's sword left to rust on the ground. As the church hierarchy calcified, Christianity began to repress women and devalue sex. Freedom was undermined, culminating in the

Crusades, the inquisitions, and the burning of witches. Some say the lights of classical science and civilization were extinguished by the church.

Like the Gnostic creator, the chief villain is given different names: John or Tertullian (in Pagels's version), Mark, Paul, Irenaeus, or Constantine. Individually or all together, these church fathers said, "There is no church besides us!" In effect, neo-Gnostic scholars reply, "You are mistaken, Oh church of the blind!"

The orthodox story of Jesus becomes in this myth what postmodern philosopher Michel Foucault called "the obligatory lies that power games and power relations presuppose."[12] The Christian Gospels were not chosen because they are truer or better in any way than Gnostic competitors. They were chosen to establish the authority of *male* church leaders.

## THE LONG SLEEP

Pagels notes that unlike other traditions, Western monotheism seldom speaks of God in feminine terms. In the East, by contrast, religion often involved a "harmonious, dynamic relationship of opposites," like *yin* and *yang*.[13] While Pagels admits that male superiority is assumed in some Gnostic texts, female figures such as Sophia, Zoe, and Mary play leading roles. The Creator is even rebuked by female divinities. Aside from such "mythical explanations," Pagels asks, "Can we find any actual, historical reasons why these Gnostic writings were suppressed?"[14] She concludes that they were excluded from the Bible because church leaders were offended by the idea of female leaders in the church. Tertullian complained that women in these heretical schools dared to teach, exorcise, heal, and maybe even baptize! After A.D. 200, under the heavy thumb of orthodoxy, female leaders were no longer permitted in the orthodox church.

Leading neo-Gnostic scholar Bart Ehrman argues that the orthodox were just one of many competing groups that "succeeded in overwhelming" other fellowships. Thus the Gnostic Gospels were excluded from the church. The orthodox then "rewrote the history of the engagement." They banished heretical books to the underworld, as it were, beneath the sands of Egypt.[15]

For a millennia and a half, Christians assumed that church dogma was the only way to interpret the story of Jesus. Some say their monotheism also encouraged the concentration of political power into the hands of kings, who saw themselves as God's anointed. The church enforced orthodoxy vigorously. But finally Sophia, or the goddess of Reason, reawoke.

## THE ENLIGHTENMENT

The Gnostic texts as a whole were lost, but fragments survived in the books that refuted them, such as Irenaeus's *Against Heresies* and Hippolytus's *Refutation of All Heresies*. This was enough to tempt the imagination of Enlightenment thinkers such as Voltaire and Gibbon. Seeing the church as oppressive and irrational, Gnostics were friends, and therefore (they assumed) liberating and rational, like themselves. Romantic poets such as William Blake and W.B. Yeats, who reacted against both Christianity and the rationalism of the Enlightenment, understood Gnosticism better, and their rage against the Christian God burned the brighter for it. ("The heavens were closed and spirits mournd their bondage day and night...Howling and Wailing fly the souls from Urizen's strong hand." "What rough beast, its hour come round at last, Slouches towards Bethlehem to be born?"—NHL: 536-7.) Then a few original sources began to turn up—fragments of *Thomas,* a large chunk of *Mary.*

The discovery of the Gnostic library in Upper Egypt has been described in almost mythological terms. These texts finally allow us, Pagels says, to hear from the other side:

> Who made that selection, and for what reasons? Why
> were these other writings excluded and banned as

"heresy"? What made them so dangerous? Now, for the first time, we have the opportunity to find out about the earliest Christian heresy; for the first time, the heretics can speak for themselves.[16]

A similar passage can be quoted from many neo-Gnostic creation accounts. Birger Pearson said Nag Hammadi allows us to read "the other side of the theological arguments we know so well from the ecclesiastical heresiologists" (NHL: 448). It seems to me though that today, the shoe is usually on the other foot. Millions read Dan Brown and his imitators, and dozens of books introduce the Gnostic Gospels. How many people today read Irenaeus? How many Hollywood directors get ideas for scripts from Justin Martyr?

Yaltabaoth shuddered when he heard the words, "You are mistaken." Neo-Gnostics also often depict orthodox Christians reacting defensively when they hear about alternative Gospels, as we will see. Some respond by burying their heads in the sand. Others choose to believe by "faith." But in the end, one may expect the censuring, banning, and burning of opposing writings.

That is a rough sketch of the neo-Gnostic myth. Like its ancient twin, it is not always clear that the people who tell this story quite believe it. Nag Hammadi authors knew their stories were untrue because they made them up. Neo-Gnostics, however, did not invent this story out of thin air. Many details can be defended, for it depends on moving the attention from the center of Christianity to late, distant, and marginal facts. The neo-Gnostic story is a shell game in which quick hand motions draw the eye from the truth about Jesus and lost Gospels to empty relativism and political speculation.

To illustrate how the game is played, and how the neo-Gnostic myth has trickled down to the general public, let's look at the hubbub surrounding two Gnostic texts. Major magazines put these texts on their covers days before and after *The Da Vinci Code* movie was released in the spring of 2006, also just after Easter (when, as Nag Hammadi general editor James Robinson pointed out, it's easiest to focus the media's attention on issues involving—or perhaps we should say, attacks on—Christianity).[17] One was a new discovery: the *Judas Gospel*, which Pagels prophesied would "change the early history of Christianity." The other was a popular text that some scholars hope can help reform modern Christianity—the *Gospel of Mary*.

## *NATIONAL GEOGRAPHIC* AND THE GOSPEL OF 30 SHEKELS

In May 2006, a photo of the *Judas Gospel* appeared on the cover of *National Geographic*. At the same time, books on *Judas* by scholars quoted or mentioned in the article showed up in stores around the world. The article and books told the dramatic story of how yet another lost manuscript had made its way through the tawdry world of the international antiquities market, speculated on the effects of the manuscript, and made the text of *Judas* available to readers, along with commentary.

*Judas* describes itself as a "secret account of the revelation that Jesus spoke in conversation with Judas Iscariot." Jesus, it says, began to speak to the disciples "about the mysteries beyond the world and what would take place at the end." The text describes a series of four interviews between Jesus and the disciples. Judas is presented not as a traitor, but the most enlightened disciple, who sold Jesus (one gathers, though the text does not spell it out) as a kind of sting operation against the devil.

*Judas* is a 12-gauge shotgun blast at orthodox Christianity. Speaking to the disciples, Jesus refers to "your god." He compares them to cannibals, homosexuals, and people who sacrifice wives or children to the devil. At the time the text was written, Christians were tortured and accused of precisely such crimes. Reading this so-called Gospel, it is not hard to see why early Christians found it difficult to swallow.

*National Geographic* solicited expert opinion from Elaine Pagels, Marvin Meyer, and Bart Ehrman, three influential neo-Gnostic scholars. Meyer is the author of numerous books on Gnostic writings. In one, he suggests that "Jesus quotes" recorded by Muslims 600 years after the life of Jesus may be accurate. While playing up the value of very late non-Christian sources in a way that few scholars would go along with, Meyer is deeply suspicious of the earliest Jesus records, the Christian Gospels. Ehrman, head of the religious studies department at the University of North Carolina, is the author of *Lost Christianities* and *Lost Scriptures*. In these works, he argues for the diversity of the early church and places the Gospels of *Thomas, Mary, Philip,* and *Truth* on the same level as the Bible. He is also a passionate former evangelical Christian. Arguing against the resurrection, Ehrman does not always contain his disagreement within the bounds of academic courtesy.[18] *National Geographic* also called on one dissenting scholar, Craig Evans, an eminent professor at Arcadia University in Nova Scotia.

The two times Evans was quoted, he zeroed in on the issue of historicity. (A matter in which he alone showed interest.) First, Evans suggested that the early Christians chose the canonical Gospels because they found them more authentic. The author of the article remarked, "Or perhaps the alternatives were simply outmaneuvered in the battle for the Christian mind"—directing the reader's attention from historical truth to power politics (an interest that Gnostics and postmodernists share). Again, Evans noted, "There is nothing in the *Gospel of Judas* that tells us anything we could consider historically reliable."[19] Rather than argue with this statement, which is unassailable, the writer quoted Pagels: "We don't look to the gospels for historical information."[20] The implication is that if we admit *Judas* is false, we must be "fair" and dump the biblical records as well. Whether equally true or equally false, *Judas* and the New Testament Gospels are consigned to the same footing, where pluralism demands they stay.

Bart Ehrman was then quoted as "agreeing" with Pagels that the discovery of *Judas* is "big," adding, "a lot of people are going to be upset."[21] At first this seems puzzling. How did Ehrman's sociological prediction about how people will react "agree" with Pagels's claim about the lack of historical value in the Gospels? Why is discovery of a text that tells us nothing true about Jesus important? And why should a document that everyone admits is pure fiction upset anyone? But Ehrman's comment supports Pagels in two ways. First, it affirms a piece of the neo-Gnostic myth that she helped create: that Gnosticism frightens Christians. And second, like Pagels's comment, it tricks unwary eyes off the question of whether *Judas* says anything *true*.

Postmodernism teaches us to be wary of the motives of historians, and here, perhaps, is a good place to begin.

The National Geographic Society spent a rumored million dollars for exclusive rights to coverage about the *Judas Gospel.* Evidently the idea that the text would upset Christians would help recover those costs. As one Amazon reviewer in the United Kingdom said of *The Da Vinci Code,* "Anything that upsets the religious right sells by the bucketful in the U.S." So Ehrman's guess about how Christians would react is reinforced not once, but three times. First, when he hears of the blasphemous text, a "Father Antony" in Egypt staggers and leans against a door to stand up. (As if to say the Christian faith does not provide this poor man with intellectual support, but at least wood still holds a body from falling through the earth.) Then the article refers briefly to Irenaeus, whose second-century *Against Heresies* is often blamed for homogenizing Christian theology. Then the article describes the suppression of heretics by the later church. So the magazine drives Ehrman's point home with three sharp blows, and affirms a good chunk of the neo-Gnostic myth along the way.

Ehrman does not try to make us think *Judas* is believable. He tries instead (as do other proponents of the myth) to use the

Gnostic writings as a broom to sweep away the canonical Gospels. All Gospels are equal, none should be privileged, and one story is as good as another. As noted earlier, Pagels says this explicitly: "We don't look to the gospels for historical information."[22] She almost certainly knows that other (and, I would say, more careful) historians do, as we will see.

So *National Geographic* chose a panel of four scholars to discuss *Judas:* three leading proponents of the Gnostic Gospel myth, and one dissident. When the dissident spoke, his comments were dismissed or rendered relative. When proponents spoke, their comments were amplified and illustrated. James Robinson, himself smitten by the neo-Gnostic bug but a careful scholar, warned that *Judas* would be used for hype. What he seemed to fear was *Da Vinci Code*-style hype—the pretense that the work is true. *National Geographic* hyped the text in a more subtle way. The article danced around the false nature of *Judas,* insinuating that reading the lightly diverting literary jabs of a second-century Alexandrian should somehow shake the foundations of Christianity. The writer then fell back to the position that if not equally true, all the Gospels must be equally false. That is one way the neo-Gnostic shell game is played.

## MARY, MARY, *AU CONTRARIE*

A few weeks later, a story on Mary Magdalene appeared on the cover of *Newsweek.* The cover showed Jesus and the person Dan Brown identifies as Mary (actually the apostle John) from Leonardo da Vinci's *The Last Supper* leaning cozily against one another. The caption read: "Beyond the Da Vinci Code: The Mystery of Mary Magdalene."

The story inside followed the neo-Gnostic myth closely. Author Anne Underwood's sources included Pagels, Ehrman, and King, who has written on Mary and the Gnostics from a somewhat more careful neo-Gnostic perspective. Unlike *National Geographic,* in 12 pages Underwood did not mention any dissidents. Much of the article read like a paraphrase of Pagels or King. (I doubt such a story would have been written by *Newsweek*'s excellent religion reporter, Kenneth Woodward.)

*Mary*, Underwood explained, is a Gnostic Gospel. The Gnostics stressed salvation "through study and self-knowledge" rather than "faith." News of these texts has turned the study of Christian origins on its head. The *Gospel of Mary* is revealing, said King, not only because it shows Mary as a "strong, willful woman," but also for its "radical ideas about gender."[23] The biblical Gospels can't avoid Mary, mentioning her 13 times, but offer few details of her life. The church found her "threatening," and "suppressed her role, and those of other women," to make the Christian priesthood a club for men, another ganglion in the Old Boys network.[24]

Mary is not mentioned in later New Testament writings. Where did she go? The Gnostics provide a troubling answer. In them, they say Mary is under constant attack, an attack that reflects the situation in the church. Pagels explains that we find two parallel traditions: one in which Peter is at the center and Mary on the sidelines, the other with Mary at the center and Peter "suspect." Peter's version survives only because church history was written by the winners.

Again, the shell master diverts attention from historical truth to power politics—in this case, with a feminist twist (we will see in a later chapter just how deceptive that twist is).

The neo-Gnostic story thus filters down from professors at major universities to mass-market novels and magazines. Elaine Pagels's myth becomes mainstream with surprisingly few questions asked.

A good one to begin with would be this: "How did first-century Christians 'suppress' stories that were not written until the second century?"

In their book on the *Gospel of Mary*, Meyer and De Boer fly in the face of that very question. Meyer argues that while the Gnostic texts give Mary a fair shake, in the New Testament, "the centrality of her role may be obscured by the interests of the authors of the Gospels, who advance the cause of the male disciples (especially the Twelve) and the place of Peter." De Boer also complains of how the New Testament "marginalizes" and "minimalizes" Mary.[25]

I find this confusing. As historians, all four of these scholars know perfectly well that the canonical Gospels precede *Mary*. In her book, King even admitted (once) that *Mary* is not historical. So all the talk about "two traditions" is smoke and mirrors. The fact that Mary "disappears" in the later New Testament means nothing. So do Jesus' parents, and so do Andrew, Nicodemus, and Lazarus. Maybe they all died. Maybe they stayed home while male disciples took the gospel to Asia and Europe (and the spotlight of canonical interest followed them). Maybe they went with Thomas to India. Nobody knows; no one should pretend to know. It is embarrassing to see serious scholars build history on such windblown vapor trails. And positively bizarre to say that earlier writings dismiss, marginalize, or obscure a literary scene that had not even been written yet. It is like saying Walt Disney purposely obscured the role Shrek would play in rescuing Sleeping Beauty.

But the neo-Gnostic myth, being a myth, is full of such leaps of logic. In the end, such scholars do not make a serious claim about Christian origins. Rather, they cause readers to doubt that there is such a thing as historical truth. They propose a cheap relativism—our gospels, their gospels, or he says, she says—and a cynical picture of the early church that puts facts with a strong historical basis on a par with pure fantasy. The dwarf Griffle would have understood. The questions, Who is the real Jesus? and Are claims to have seen Jesus political ploys? really come down to, Who can we trust, and why should we trust them? These are good questions, if asked honestly. But the cynic who tells us, without evidence, that all religions are equally false is demagoguing as surely as the bumbler who counts them all equally true.

# 4

# THERE ARE NO GNOSTIC GOSPELS

IN THE HANS CHRISTIAN ANDERSEN story *The Ugly Duckling,* an odd-looking chick is born in the nest of a mother duck. Picked on for his large size and awkward gait, he sets out on a journey on which he finally learns that he is not a duck, but rather a swan.

What sort of bird are Gnostic stories about Jesus? Do they belong to the same species of literature as the biblical Gospels? The question is not just semantic; we must understand what these books really are.

Novelist Madeleine L'Engle said a book title is "as important as one's right and proper signature on a check."[1] *The Gnostic Gospels* was a huge publishing and critical success, winning the National Book Critics Circle Award and also inspiring serious scholars. Other scholars also signed on to the idea with titles such as *The Five Gospels, The Complete Gospels, Secret Teachings of Jesus: Four Gnostic Gospels, The Gospel of Mary, The Gospel of Philip,* and *The Judas Gospel.* Even titles that don't use the word *Gospel* often make the same point in another way, such as Bart Ehrman's *Lost Scriptures.* Dan Brown claimed there were more than 80 Gospels, and Meyer said there were 30.

Clearly, the word *Gospel* is important. A true Gospel tells us who Jesus is, shows us the face of God, as it were, and explains why we are here.

Calling the Nag Hammadi writings Gospels not only sells books, but is meant to take the biblical Gospels down a peg or two. Holy Scripture, or at least our best sources for the life of Jesus, become items for sale on the shelf marked "Gospels." But the neo-Gnostics are passing forged checks. They ask, "Isn't it time to hear the other side of the story from alternative Gospels gathered piece by piece from the rubbish bin of 'approved' history?" The appeal is democratic and clever; but as we will see, it completely confuses the nature of these texts. *Gospel* has become another linguistic shell that is used to trick unwary eyes away from the truth.

## THREE WAYS OF DEFINING WORDS

Words are defined by the meanings of their parts and by how they are used. Their core meaning is then often extended by analogy.

For example, the word *Bible* is from the Greek *biblia,* or "the books," plural of *biblion.* It derives from the Semitic *biblos,* meaning "papyrus," or scroll. For us, it means the collection of sacred texts that includes the Torah, prophets, wisdom literature, Gospels, and epistles. We call this collection the Bible, because Christians see it as the source of all God has revealed about the creation and the nature of the Creator, virtue and sin, redemption and salvation.

This basic meaning is often extended by analogy. On Amazon.com you can find a *Barbecue Bible, Wine Bible, Wedding Bible,* and *LSAT Logical Reasoning Bible.* One assumes these volumes do for the taste buds, nuptials, or mental faculties what the Bible does for the soul. We expect some poetic extension (hype) from publishers, though. And like wineskins, words assume new shapes as they stretch to hold the "new wine" of a metaphorical title. We don't expect psalms in praise of drumsticks in the *Barbecue Bible,* or an apocalypse at the end of what could be called *The Body-Building Bible*—unless maybe it were written by Governor Ahnold!

Do the root meaning and common use of *Gospel* fit the Nag Hammadi stories about Jesus? Or is the term *Gnostic Gospels* like the *Barbecue Bible*—just hype that helps sell books and ideas?

## DEFINING *GOSPEL*

*Gospel* derives from the old English *gods spel,* from the Greek *euangelion. Eu* means "good." *Eugenics* is "good breeding." *Euphoria* is "a good feeling." J.R.R. Tolkien coined the term *eucatastrophe* to designate the "good disaster" at the climax of a fairy tale, when the dragon is slain, or Gandalf the White returns. *Angelion* means "news." So *euangelion* means "good news."

But *Gospel* does not mean just any good news—such as a newspaper story that announces your team won, a favorable earnings report, or a voice message from a girl saying yes, she would like to go out for pizza. Nor do we usually talk about the Gospel of Krishnamurti or the Gospel of Mohammed. *Gospel* meant good news about something the Hebrew Creator did for all mankind through a man named Jesus.

Dictionaries make this clear. One defines *Gospel* as "the story of Christ's life and teachings, especially as contained in the first four books of the New Testament," or "any of these four books."[2] Another defines how this core meaning can be extended: "One of the first four New Testament books telling of the life, death, and resurrection of Jesus Christ, *also, a similar apocryphal book.*"[3] If a book closely resembles the biblical books of Matthew, Mark, Luke, or John, we might legitimately call it a Gospel. But if it looks nothing like them, standard definitions give no reason to call it a Gospel.

So we face three questions. First, do Gnostic writings fit the root meaning of Gospel? Are they "good news"? Second, do any look like the first four New Testament books? And third, if neither is the case, can we still extend the meaning of *Gospel* by analogy, as with *Barbecue Bible?*

## THE SEARCH FOR GOOD NEWS

The answer to the first question is clearly no. The most famous Gnostic text, the *Gospel of Thomas*, is a collection of 114 mostly metaphysical sayings. It does not contain a single line of what any journalist would call news. *Gospel of Truth* is a sermon, and so, in its own way, is *Gospel of the Egyptians.* The Gospels of *Mary, Philip,* and *Judas* do tell stories about Jesus, but the emphasis of each one is on the Gnostic myth, not on anything Jesus does.

The truth is, the Gnostic writings show no interest in the past. They mention a few folks and events from Jewish history. But the people are more like Robin Hood than the Internal Revenue Service—symbols, not real-world characters. And not even the latest episode mentioned—the sacking of Jerusalem in A.D. 70—was news to anyone by the time the Gnostic Gospels were written. And Jesus did not die. Not having died, he probably (it's a bit hazy) didn't come to life again. He taught eternal truths and is vaguely said to have worked miracles. But he has left history and entered mythological time.

It is hard to find news at Nag Hammadi, let alone good news.

## DOES IT QUACK LIKE A DUCK?

Our second question is this: Do any of the Gnostic writings resemble the canonical Gospels in the Bible? Obviously some people think they do. Dan Brown built an empire on the premise that there are secret Gospels. Scholars have built their reputations and undermined Christianity by talking about the Gnostic Gospels. One would think someone had found one. In fact, no one has.

The legend of 30 to 80 Gospels arises from two superficial facts: that a few Gnostic books borrow the title, and that about two dozen of these books refer to names and events from the biblical Gospels.

Like roll call at a Columbian prison, at first the names seem biblical, but the banter sounds all wrong. Why does Jesus laugh when people suffer? Why does he ramble on about cosmic sex, pleromas, aeons, and archons? How come he tells followers not to heal people? Why doesn't anyone go fishing?

But we're told we shouldn't judge a book by its cover, or a few scattered phrases. So I dug deeper. I carefully analyzed the Christian Gospels, finding 50 characteristics that they almost always share. It is as if Jesus left fingerprints on the biblical writings. Like fingerprints or DNA, the Gospels reveal a personality profile, a pattern so specific that they render Jesus distinct from any other person. Then I analyzed the most popular Gnostic writing, the *Gospel of Thomas,* in the same way.

I'll share five comparisons that reveal just how deep the divide is between the biblical Gospels and the Gnostic Gospels.

## JESUS, PRISONER OF TIME AND PLACE?

First, the canonical Gospels of the Bible are firmly set in time, place, and culture. Jesus broiled fish from the Sea of Galilee, taught on a hill overlooking the lake, confronted a lynch mob in Capernaum, was baptized in the Jordan River, and prayed at the Mount of Olives. Even Pagels admitted, "All of the New Testament gospels, whatever their differences, concern themselves with Jesus as a historical person."[4]

That historical person is Jewish. Jesus answers questions about God and his kingdom, the law, and the Messiah from the Hebrew Scriptures; he knows them well. Even the most Christian teachings in the New Testament are intensely Jewish. Jesus is compared to the Passover lamb, the snake Moses hoisted on a pole in the wilderness, and the lamb Isaiah spoke of that refused to bleat while being sheared. He is the long-awaited Son of David. He is the temple, God among us. On Mount Moriah, God promised to bless all the peoples of the world through the seed of Abraham. The Jews believed in a political and spiritual Messiah who would rule the nations and bring justice to the world. Here, the Gospels say, was that seed. Christ would rule in the hearts of his disciples. Jesus does not wander aimlessly from place to place "on a never-ending picnic," as G.K. Chesterton described the life of the late first-century sage Apollonius.[5] He is drawn toward the urban heart of his faith as if into a vortex: "Can a prophet die outside of Jerusalem?" (see Luke 13:33). The Gospels tease new meaning from every layer of the Old Testament like a gardener nursing vegetable seeds into a summer banquet. Even the "carnal" Jewish hope for physical salvation is affirmed when Jesus rose from the dead.

By contrast, the Gnostic Gospels seldom—if ever—touch down on *terra firma*. *Thomas* says "twenty-four prophets spoke in Israel." Some mention Old Testament figures such as Adam, Eve, Noah, or Moses. But such occasional bits of local color only underscore how non-Jewish these books are. It is like opening a story about hippies in India by saying, "Kirsten popped acid in Goa, and experienced *kundalini* awakening." Even the setting is cosmic, which is why cosmic boredom sets in.

A lot of academic dust has been kicked up over whether, like the chicken or the egg, the biblical Gospels or *Thomas* came first. Most scholars say *Thomas* was written in the second century, though some claim a core goes back to the first, perhaps even before the biblical Gospels. As I researched the question, I noticed though that "early *Thomas*" scholars did not always bother to interact with contrary arguments. In her book *Beyond Belief*, for example, Elaine Pagels trashed the Gospel of John with arguments that would badly fail if his Gospel came before *Thomas*. Yet she never mentioned that such eminent scholars as N.T. Wright,

John Meier, Richard Hays, or Phillip Jenkins have argued strongly against an early *Thomas*. In fact, she did not admit there was a controversy at all.

When Pagels came to Seattle, I asked her what she thought of arguments by Wright and Meier that *Thomas* was late. She said they were "excellent scholars," but admitted she had not read their arguments against her position.

I was shocked. I'm still shocked. Here was a famous Princeton historian undermining Christianity before large, enthusiastic audiences who saw her as The Expert, admitting, after a solid hour of signing books, that she had not done what I ask undergraduate academic writing students to do. She had not read contrary arguments. Reading both sides of the debate, I came to the conclusion that the majority of scholars are right: *Thomas* is late. I also concluded that some "ex spurts" are spouting when they should still be drinking.

Not even Pagels claims, though, that any Gnostic text shows discernable ties to the persons, places, or ideas of first-century Israel.

## HE "CASTS OUT DEMONS ONLY BY...THE RULER OF THE DEMONS"[6]

Another remarkable quality of the biblical Gospels is how roughly people treat the Master. Jesus is subject to nit-picking, suspicion, entrapment, barbed comments, and angry denunciations. He is accused of being a commoner, sinner, Samaritan, and demon, and of breaking Jewish law, not paying taxes, lacking education, blasphemy, insanity, and black magic. The Gospels also show how he is whipped, spit upon, and killed.

The Gospels describe a series of confrontations between Jesus and opponents leading up to the crucifixion. Key people become suspicious. Who does this rabbi think he is? His healings seem impressive, but has he forgotten the divine law against work on the Sabbath? And why is this "holy man" mixing with such shady characters? Opposition grows, and gets testy. That parable about the elder son meant us, didn't it? And the story of the vineyard—is he accusing us of killing the prophets? The mob grows unruly. Who in Sheol does this man think he is? How dare he claim that the words of the prophets are fulfilled by some bumpkin preacher from Galilee! Powerful leaders begin to discuss what to do. The conflict is as dramatic and gritty with reality as the last days of Malcolm X as described by Alex Haley.

By contrast, Jesus gets a pass in Gnostic writings. He is called "wise philosopher" *(Thomas)*, a "righteous angel" *(Thomas)*, and "the illuminator" *(The Letter of Peter to Paul)*, who "has everything in himself: man, angel, mystery, and the Father" *(Gospel of Philip)*. He never cries. He does laugh, but as we will see, it is not a humanizing laughter. He is the Teflon Savior, hated by evil archons, seemingly crucified and "buried in a tomb," but really a "stranger to this suffering" (*Letter of Peter to Paul*, NHL: 436).

## GOOD TEACHER?

Third, in the Gospels, Jesus teaches us to love one another. This may seem obvious—so obvious that critics don't notice how different the Nag Hammadi Gospels are.

Jesus belonged to the "tough love" school of counseling. He told his followers repeatedly to take up their crosses. "Stop sinning or something worse will happen!" "You've had five husbands and the bloke you're living with now isn't one!" "Vipers! Who told you to flee from the wrath of hell?" His teachings shock and challenge people of every time and culture. "If someone slaps you on the cheek, turn to him the other." "Sell everything you have and come follow me." "Don't lust." "Be perfect, like your Father in heaven."

Yet many of Jesus' teachings are surprisingly humble and mild. They would embarrass a Jain, ready to fast to death for enlightenment, or Siddhartha, who ate only a few grains of rice a day. Jesus said, "Produce good fruit." "Feed my lambs." "Do not make my

Father's house a house of business." "Do good on the Sabbath." "Give a cup of water in the name of the Lord." "No need to fast while the bridegroom is here!" "Drink wine to remember me." What all these teachings reveal is an earthiness and practicality to Jesus, along with a passion for the radical love of God.

The crowds around Jesus said, "No one ever taught like this man" (see John 7:46). Great modern thinkers agree. "No one has taught as Jesus Christ," Chinese philosopher Lin Yutang concluded after spending a lifetime poring over and enjoying the genius of world literature.[7]

Gnostic authors did not even try to compete. On the contrary, the Nag Hammadi corpus shows a deep-seated, almost pathological dislike for moral teaching. My claim may offend some readers, but it is true.

I first noticed the Gnostic attitude when I compared *Thomas* and Q, a hypothetic document that some think was used by both Luke and Matthew when they wrote their Gospels. Jesus Seminar scholars call both works "sayings Gospels" and seem to think they are much alike. The in-house publishing organ of the Jesus Seminar, Polebridge Press, even produced a *Q-Thomas Reader* on the theory that the two were the earliest Gospels. Q includes much of the Sermon on the Mount, the richest body of moral teaching in human thought, which thrilled Mahatmas Gandhi and caused Leo Tolstoy agony as he tried to live up to it. I found that between 37 and 55 percent of Q, as defined by the Jesus Seminar, teaches ethics in one way or other.

Almost all this is edited out of *Thomas*.[8] Jesus grudgingly tells the disciples to heal the sick, but warns them not to give to the poor for fear they will harm their spirits. Only two percent of *Thomas* is about doing good, directly or indirectly. That sets the book apart not only from the genuine Gospels, but from every canonical text in the Bible.

Studying other Nag Hammadi texts, I found lack of passion for compassion to be a defining characteristic of the whole body of literature. If anything, *Thomas* is better than most. Few Gnostic texts are comprised of even one percent moral teachings. Out of about 13,000 lines in English, I found only 80 that had to do with morality—about 0.6 percent. What's more, the few scattered references to kindness, courage, or forgiveness are never original or inspiring. "The perfect Father is good" (NHL: 65). "He who does injustice truly does not profit" (NHL: 319—from Plato!). "In haughtiness they shall grasp at pride" (NHL: 375). Such half-hearted platitudes are like withered shrubs in a vast and empty desert. In all of the Nag Hammadi Library, I have not found a single thoughtful teaching about how to live a virtuous life.

Remarkably, I have also yet to find any neo-Gnostic scholar who comments on this fact. This is particularly startling because scholars such as Robert Funk, John Crossan, Marcus Borg, and Elaine Pagels are alive to the radical nature of Jesus' moral teachings. Yet they promote *Thomas,* which edits out every trace of Jesus' kindness, as a Fifth Gospel! Or maybe it is the first. Certainly *Thomas* is the latest thing in Christian insight.

Lack of moral concern alone shows why no Gnostic writing should be called a Gospel, defined, as we saw, as the "story of Christ's life *and teachings.*" One might also wonder why the appearance of so inconsiderate a person as the Gnostic Jesus is supposed to be good news.

## SOCIAL GOSPEL

Jesus was not a teacher of abstract ethical codes; he was a people person. He was sensitive to the needs of others. He welcomed children. Jesus was "a man of sorrow, and acquainted with grief," but also the life of some very interesting parties. His stories are "full of eating, drinking, and making merry."[9] And he practiced what he preached, defying social codes by dining with tax collectors and prostitutes. He began public ministry at a wedding and ended it at a banquet with close friends.

As has been said of the biologist Steven Jay Gould, Jesus had a gift for noticing things—not about artifacts, but about people. His disciples would see members of a class: blind beggar, tax collector, Gentile, Samaritan, woman. But Jesus always noticed people: a lady who had taken it on the chin from the medical profession, a man with strong spiritual vision who lived in a world of physical darkness, a woman with a history of failed relationships who hungered for God, Zacchaeus the Short.

Jesus "routinely breached the walls and barriers that set sacred space off from profane, and he trampled indifferently on the social dividers that enforced segregation,"[10] said Funk. Even in his stories, half-breeds, tax collectors, and beggars turned out to be heroes.

You won't find this side of Jesus in any Gnostic text, either. Rather, Jesus is aloof from suffering, and even from his disciples. In *Judas,* he seems to detest them. Elsewhere he tolerates them as props, like sidekicks in a radio talk show who exist to bring out "the talent's" wisdom. At times he imparts that wisdom reluctantly, making it clear that he would rather shuffle off this mortal popsicle stand and return to the pleroma. As for outsiders, Jesus doesn't even talk to them, let alone go to their parties.

## GOD AND GOSPEL

Finally, of the nine theological characteristics that I found to define the Gospels, let me touch briefly on miracles. N.T. Wright pointed out that the miraculous works of Jesus do not at all "protrude" from the rest of the narrative, but "fit remarkably well into the complete picture of Jesus' ministry."[11] Jesus' miracles almost always followed a highly specific and distinct pattern. They were *realistic, purposeful, constructive, respectful,* and *pious,* in the sense of pointing people to God. Jesus did not levitate, make stained glass windows bleed, pull chicken organs out of people's stomachs, or create holy ash or *lingams,* the stone sex organs favored by some Indian gurus. He met real people with real needs—a woman who had been bleeding for 12 years, a quick-witted blind man, a paralyzed man with world-class friends and a crowbar. He looked them in the eye and spoke and acted like a friend.

Again, pore over the Gnostic texts and look for any trace of this Jesus. A few of them mention that he did miracles. But that's just elevator music. Miracles are another part of the good news that did not fit the Nag Hammadi palate.

## WHAT GNOSTIC GOSPELS?

Over the last several pages, I feel like I've been trying to write an outline of the human genome sequence with a stubby pencil. The Gospels contain libraries of deeply meaningful truth tightly coiled in words like genes in a strand of DNA. A few words—such as "give to Caesar the things that are Caesar's, and to God the things that are God's," and "turn the other cheek"—have colossal consequences in the real world.

Scholars often remark on how clever and sophisticated the Gnostics were. Irenaeus admitted, "They run us down as utterly contemptible and ignorant persons." It sometimes looks as if a Zen Master has been at *Thomas, Thunder, Perfect Mind,* or the *Gospel of Truth:* There is lyricism here, and hints of profundity. *Judas* and *Mary* contain some biting satire, at least. But in all the Nag Hammadi Library, I do not think you can find a single saying from the mouth of Jesus, or a single scene in his life, that make an observant reader think, *Jesus is here.*

In detailed analysis, I found that *Thomas* shared between five and seven traits with the Gospels—three having to do with how Jesus taught. This was less than any other ancient writing I examined. That is remarkable, because none of the other books—*Iliad, Agricola* by Tacitus, the Babylonian *Epic of Gilgamesh,* the stories of Hercules, the Chinese martial arts romance *Journey to the West,* and the earliest stories about Confucius—is called a Gospel. None mentions Jesus, the God of Israel, or even the land of Palestine. If Gospel is a writing that looks like the New Testament books, then almost every ancient book is more of a Gospel than the best lost "Gospel" from the sands of Egypt. Whether we go by root meaning or ordinary usage, no such thing as a Gnostic Gospel has been found.

But can we extend the meaning of the word by analogy? Sure. If there is a *Barbecue Bible*, there can be Gnostic Gospels, too. And that is how the word is used: as an advertising gimmick, a sales charm, a verbal trick to help make "good news" for a publisher in San Francisco or Washington, DC. The technical term for an ancient book ascribed to someone other than the real author is *pseudopigrapha*, or "falsely attributed writing." The National Geographic Society could hardly recoup a million dollar investment by promoting the *Judas Pseudopigrapha*.

Does it matter if you call a rose a thistle, or a thistle a rose?

I believe it does. Calling the Gnostic texts Gospels is confusing in the literal sense of fusing with, or joining, things that are not like each other.

Words either point to the truth, or away from it. If semantics can hide the truth about the Gnostic Gospels, straight talk reveals that the biblical Gospels are unique, and so is the person whom they introduce.

During the 1988 U.S. presidential campaign, the vice presidential candidates, the patriarchal Lloyd Bentsen and the youthful-looking Dan Quayle, had an revealing exchange. Quayle made the mistake of comparing himself to former president John F. Kennedy. Bentsen retorted cuttingly: "Senator, I served with Jack Kennedy. I knew Jack Kennedy. Jack Kennedy was a friend of mine. But I can tell you this, senator: you're no Jack Kennedy."[12]

This may seem a bit harsh. Kennedy was a charismatic president whose assassination put him almost beyond criticism. But he was also a flawed man whose presidency was not in every respect a success. Quayle seemed a decent person, even if he couldn't spell *potatoes.* However, Quayle was guilty of presumption in comparing himself, even implicitly, to Kennedy. Such overreach was rightly seen as significant. It was also a strategic error to draw attention to a comparison so unlikely to flatter him.

Gnostics and their heirs are guilty of much greater presumption. You don't need to be a great historian, such as Wright or Meier, to feel the presumption of calling *Thomas* or *Philip* a Gospel. Anyone who knows the Bible well, and who reads Nag Hammadi texts, has every right to respond: "Professor, I read the New Testament. I know the New Testament. The Jesus of the Gospels is a friend of mine. I can tell you this, professor: these are not Gospels. This metaphysics-spouting mystic from Upper Egypt is no Jesus."

# "GNOSTIC CHRISTIANITY" IS A CONTRADICTION IN TERMS

IN THE LAST CHAPTER, I argued that it makes no sense to call any known Gnostic writing a Gospel. Talking about a *Gospel of Thomas* or *Gospel of Mary* confuses the nature both of the biblical Gospels and the Gnostic writings.

Some scholars are even more insistent about saying the Gnostics were Christian. The term *Gnostic Christian* appears frequently in Pagels's work, especially as she describes how the orthodox circled the wagons to keep Gnostics and others outside, to the loss of Western civilization. This is also the theme of Bart Ehrman's *Lost Christianities*. Ehrman ponders, "The empire might have converted to *a different form of Christianity* and the development of Western society and culture might have developed in ways we cannot imagine."[1] Karen King seems offended by the suggestion that some Gnostics were not Christian. Early Christians are often depicted as narrow-minded and shortsighted for denying (as they did) that these good folks were Christian in any real sense.

"And should we label people at all?" some might ask. "What right do you have to say who is or isn't a Christian? Isn't that where the Christian church took its wrong turn? Isn't this business of defining religious 'ins' and 'outs' what leads to inquisitions?"

We do, I agree, need to tread carefully. I think the Christian faith gives excellent practical advice for how to do so. But I will argue that it is necessary to define, as the early Christians did, what Christianity is and is not. If we think about the issue honestly, it is absurd, for several reasons, to call Gnostics *Christian.* As with the term *Gospel,* the real question is why the pretense is made.

## THE CASE FOR DIVERSITY

The best argument for calling Gnostics *Christian* is social. Let me make the case on the microscopic level. Some believe evolution sometimes occurs when viruses bring new genetic information into a one-celled organism. If the cell says, "Virus, begone!" it may lose out on genes that will give it a crucial advantage in the struggle for life. By excluding Gnosticism, neo-Gnostics feel, the church lost a great deal of worthwhile "genetic information," such as mysticism, a healthier view of women, and skepticism about hierarchy.

Modern books on Gnosticism are often hymns to diversity. This is understandable: A healthy society is an open society. Clement of Alexander pointed out that Greco-Roman civilization borrowed ideas from three dozen or so different cultures. No one who enjoys food can dispute Clement's point: What would Italian food be without tomatoes from Peru? How would Americans celebrate the Fourth of July without watermelons ("western melon") from China?

Pagels pointed out that two early critics of Gnosticism, Hippolytus and Tertullian, joined "heretical" splinter groups in later years and attacked the Catholic church with the gusto once used against Gnostics. Christian history became an orgy of anathemas. Sects pounded away at one another for 1400 years, then Martin Luther tacked his 95 theses to the Wittenberg door and fractured the church into a thousand pieces. Religious war soon ravaged much of Europe. The trouble begins, one could argue, when someone else's church father becomes my heretic.

But, of course, viruses are often harmful. Later we will see that the "genetic package" Gnosticism brings is, too. But for now I want to concentrate on the practical value of labels.

Pagels spoke of Gnostic Christians and orthodox Christians. Some, however, think even these terms are unfair. Helmut Koester and James Robinson argue that the terms *orthodox, heretical, canonical,* and *non-canonical* are all obsolete. Karen King agrees, pointing out that the Gnostics did not call themselves Gnostics. All such terms were used "to identify the winners and losers in inner-Christian debate." Tellingly, however, all three scholars use these terms themselves.[2]

## THE CASE FOR LABELING HERETICS

All speech involves labeling. This is why even those who frown on labels generally use them. Boundaries around every group are fuzzy. It can be hard to define who exactly is or is not a communist, a gardener, a parent, a Buddhist, or a Christian. But however imprecise and ambiguous words may be, it is harder to communicate without them!

History is full of hatreds, and haters do fix labels: to say who is welcome and who is not, to mark off forbidden territory, and finally to paint an enemy camp with lasers for attack. In Russia, the word *communist* came to mean "clear-thinking and responsible person," while in America, it meant, roughly, "someone who wants to destroy all that is holy."

The danger of reducing a person's character to a label and simplistically dismissing him on that basis is real. But labeling is necessary for clarity of thought, and is also a sign of life.

Consider the cell again. Everything that lives must define what is or is not itself. While there are beneficial viruses, in general, if a cell membrane is compromised, life chemicals seep out and pathogens creep in. Likewise, the best national security has always been a tall mountain range, a wide desert, or better yet, an ocean to mark the national boundary. "Good fences make good neighbors." A key test of every faith is to clearly define itself and still love and respect the humanity of those outside.

*Gnosticism* is a good tag for the dominant worldview of the communities that produced the Nag Hammadi texts. Almost all these texts speak of a *gnosis*—a divinely revealed knowledge that leads to salvation. Christians find salvation in Christ. Inner knowledge plays the same role in Gnosticism, so that's a good way to define it. Jesus may or may not show up, which hardly matters because it isn't Jesus anyway—just a useful mouthpiece.

The early Christians had an idea of diversity that I believe helps resolve the tension between the need for openness and the need for clarity and safety.

We are told the early Christian community was diverse. So it was. Followers of Jesus quickly formed a multicultural community that included the powerful and slaves, men and even more women, and a phenomenal burst of cultures. "In Christ," said Paul, "there is neither Jew nor Greek, slave nor free, male nor female." He didn't mean these people couldn't be found in the church, but that they could, and before God and one another, the differences didn't matter. What counted was not the color, shape, or adornment of the nose, but where it pointed. James rebuked church greeters who seated the rich in box seats while shuffling the poor towards the nosebleed section of the sanctuary: "Did not God choose the poor of this world to be rich in faith and heirs of the kingdom...?" (James 2:5). The lowly should be proud of their "high position," and the wealthy of their "humble place."

Bishop Agobard of Lyons said that in the early church, "all men are brothers, all invoke one same Father, God: the slave and the master, the poor man and the rich man, the ignorant and the learned, the weak and the strong." Luke named 15 languages that the disciples spoke at Pentecost. The New Testament was quickly translated into many of them.

The gospel was clearly defined, however.

Paul's image for illustrating diversity was the human body, in which different, specialized organs work together in harmony. How should parts in the "body of Christ" get along? By "speaking the truth in love" (Ephesians 4:15). That's the magic formula. Be completely honest, but care about the person you are honest to. Orthodoxy set firm boundaries between truth and error but demanded that believers love those outside. After all, Christians shared two fundamental qualities with their neighbors: All were created in the image of God (no talk of spiritual or carnal essences here), and we are all sinners (which is why we need to be reminded to do right, sometimes with a touch of fire and brimstone).

Some forms of diversity improve things, others don't. A song with all the same notes is "mono-tonous." Life is richer when we can listen to Balinese folk music in the afternoon, eat Punjabi samosas for dinner, and watch Shakespeare in the park toward dusk. On the other hand, blood lubricates the circulatory system best—not catsup, soy sauce, or even first-class Burgundy.

Modern society is confused because it does not distinguish between diversity that creates and diversity that destroys. We "tolerate" one another because religion is no longer about truth. Therefore unity is not a unity of mind, heart, or soul, but skin deep.

Everything that has a function—vein, go-cart, trombone—works best in some ways and not others. We praise religious diversity because we have forgotten what faith is for. Religion is not ornamental. It is the search for ultimate truth, love, life, and beauty. And so a faith that lies, encourages hatred, spreads gloom, or creates ugliness is not equally true or even equally useful.

For neo-Gnostics, to "be in Christ" seems to mean sharing the word *Christ,* even if we mean completely different things by it. *God* may just as well mean "the devil who created this hellhole of a world." *Christ* can mean "an uncreated entity who possessed the body of Jesus to stick it to the Jewish God and teach us how to ascend to the eighth heaven." This is like thinking the citizens of Cairo, Egypt and Cairo, Georgia share a water source because they share the same town name. The truth is, they don't even share a continent.

So for the sake of clarity, and also because truth matters, it is legitimate to ask if Gnostics were real Christians. If not, we must also remember that Jesus demands that we love our enemies.

## WHY GNOSTICS WERE NOT CHRISTIAN

Gnosticism was not Christian for six reasons.

First, Gnosticism could not be Christian because it was not Jewish.

In *Thomas,* Duke scholar Richard Hays explained, the teachings of Jesus about the kingdom of God "have been removed from their native content in Jewish apocalyptic thought and converted into teachings about secret heavenly knowledge."[3] The parables, said Wright, have been "shorn of their allegorical, and Israel-specific, elements," in favor of a "radically Hellenized worldview."[4] King admitted the same about *Mary:* "The theology of *The Gospel of Mary* shows almost no ties to Judaism."[5] The Gnostic Jesus compares worshiping the Jewish God to cannibalism, for heaven's sake! How could something so hateful of Judaism be Christian, when love of the Father overflows the Gospels, and Jesus came to fulfill the Hebrew faith? As a tree grows from its roots, universal Christian truth struck a taproot deep in the soil of Israel.

At times, the Gnostic Jesus sounds suspiciously like another pompous Greek metaphysician, Apollonius of Tyana. "I come of myself, if possible to make men of you, in spite of yourselves!" "I must go my way where Science and a higher Power guide me!"

Second, it's unreasonable to call something *Christian* when it leaves out Christ, the Messiah promised in the Old Testament.

Gnostic texts sometimes use *Christ* and *Savior* like other magic monikers, such as *Sophia, Logos, Adamas,* but are careless of their meaning.

*Christ* is, by definition, more than a messenger or even a guide. Every first-century Christian writer saw Jesus as the Deliverer promised by God to save his people from their sins. But Pagels tells us one of the key insights of Gnosticism is that we save ourselves.[6] Then what do we need a Savior for? One gets the feeling, again, that verbal shells are being used to distract us from matter-of-fact truth.

Third, as we saw in the last chapter, and will see more in the next, the Gnostic Jesus is a quite different person.

Fourth, some scholars claim Jesus taught a form of Gnosticism, but early Christian records show he didn't. The first Christian teachings are found in the New Testament and (a bit later) in works such as the *Didache,* the *Letter of Clement,* and *Shepherd of Hermas.* Not one of these is Gnostic. The Gnostics referred to themselves as "the few," which they always seem to have been. Nag Hammadi writings themselves often quote the New (and Old) Testament, offering backhanded testimony to the fact that they were already authoritative.

Walter Baur and Helmut Koester famously argued that the original form of Christianity in Egypt was Gnostic. But the evidence is that Christian Gnosticism only appeared *after* orthodoxy, and grew from it like fungus on a tree. Only one of fourteen second-century Scripture fragments found in Egypt is Gnostic. Seven were from the Old Testament, which Gnostics would never use.[7]

Other neo-Gnostic scholars make much of the fact that the exact list of the 27 books now included in the New Testament was not proposed until the fourth century. The canon was not fixed until so late, so we are asked to believe (by Bart Ehrman, for example) that all "Scriptures" written before the canon were on a par, like walk-on candidates at a baseball tryout. Nothing could be further from the truth. Everyone in the mid-second century knew which books were the "stars." Already by A.D. 140 at the latest, the four Gospels were accepted as authoritative. They were widely quoted, even by Gnostics. The canon was not fixed, it is true, but all that means is that people were still unsure about a few minor works, such as 2 Peter.

All these facts show that orthodoxy was not undeveloped until the fourth century, as so often claimed. Gnostics came out of or reacted against an orthodox faith that was already well established by the fourth century.

In his book *Pre-Christian Gnosticism,* Edwin Yamauchi showed that "all of the evidence" for a Gnosticism before Christianity is actually from later sources. "Gnosticism always appears as a parasite," he concluded. The case for an early Gnosticism is "little more than an elaborate, multi-storied, many-roomed house of cards, whose foundations have been shaken...."[8]

Fifth, even if other communities could make some claim to the title *Christian* at some time in the past, surely the statute of limitations has run out by now! Language is set by use, and for 2000 years, *Christian* (and its equivalents in other languages) has meant "orthodoxy."

Mohammed probably had a better theological claim to be called a Christian. The Muslim prophet also talked about Jesus. And unlike the Gnostics, he believed in a good Creator, and (in theory) most of what the Jews said about him. The Jesus of Muslim tradition answered enemies kindly, did acts of compassion, and taught disciples to care for others.[9] We don't call Mohammed a Christian, however, in part because he rejected Christian teachings.

Definition need not be an act of hostility or intolerance: It is the act of semiotic talent by which human beings mark the boundary between life and nonlife. It is thought in the service of life. Faith communities, like organisms, exist by admitting selectively. In fact, the most successful religions are often those that make it difficult to join.[10] Why call a religion that was anti-Jewish, did not preach Christ, ignored what Christ preached, said God was the devil, and we save ourselves *Christian* contrary to 2000 years of habit? The word *Christian* can be used as a kind of hostile takeover bid, a maneuver designed to puncture the integrity of the Christian faith.

But Nag Hammadi is on the Nile River, not the Jordan. Gnosticism relates more closely to mainstream pagan religions that flow out of three great pagan civilizations: Egypt, Greece, and India.

## GNOSTICS AND POLYTHEISM

Like most ideological startups, Gnosticism borrowed "capital" from established spiritual corporations. The popular imagination of the time, Gnostic included, seemed filled with Homer and Hercules as well as Plato. Archons seduce or rape Eve like Zeus pursuing a comely maiden. The higher beings are themselves the product of cosmic copulation. The Gnostics engaged in channeling or shamanism. One text suggests some gods have frog (male) and cat (female) faces. Gnostic texts sometimes feature cameo appearances by Greek (Zeus, Aphrodite, Hermes) and Egyptian (Ammon, Tat) gods.

The Gnostics also invented two new categories of divine beings: *aeons* and *archons.* Like the Muses or Fates, their names personified virtues. In *Zostrianos,* the hero is baptized several times by aeonic entities—such as Wisdom, Self-Generated, Repentance—each time gaining better positions in the divine order. All this has a bureaucratic feel to it that tastes familiar to a student of Chinese spiritualism. Heaven borrows its personnel flowchart from imperial politics.

## GNOSTICS AND PLATO

As we saw, the Gnostic myth closely follows the characters and plot of Plato's allegory of the cave: slaves, slavemasters, instructors, ascent. The quintessential Platonic idea that earthly objects are copies of heavenly forms was also adopted by the Gnostics: People and animals correspond to heavenly, and immortal, master copies. The worlds are copies of aeons, Eve of Divine Wisdom, and the mortal Jesus is a copy of Adamas, her consort.

## GNOSTICS AND EASTERN RELIGION

*The Catholic Encyclopedia* online calls Gnosticism "markedly peculiar" for seeking salvation through "mysteries" and ritual magic rather than obedience to the gods and good works. Not so peculiar, I think. Hinduism and Buddhism also promise salvation through inner enlightenment.

A friend who follows the Hindu guru Muktananda pointed to Gnostic writings as proof that Jesus was "one of them." It is indeed possible to read the Nag Hammadi Library and conclude that Jesus was adept in "eastern religion." (I put the term in quotation marks because there is much in Asian religion that is very different, and sometimes closer to Christianity, than what we normally call "eastern religion."[11])

The Gnostic God has no desire. He is unknowable, indescribable, and untouchable. Sometimes a spiritual person seems to *become* God. The Father "dwells" within all the powers, or even within "every movement that exists in all matter." Each aeon is a "power and property" of the Father, "intermingled and harmonious." Those who come from the Father do not separate, but "become him as well." I quoted a passage from the Hindu *Upanishads* that expresses similar ideas. You can also find them in the *Bhagavad Gita* and the Buddhist *Lotus Sutra.*

Along with pantheism and henotheism, Gnostics shared with philosophical Hindus and Buddhists the belief that matter defiles us. One poet summarized the Gnostic view in an image similar to the Buddhist picture of the lotus flower growing from grime:

"You walked in mud, and your garments were not soiled" (NHL: 263). So Gnosticism resembled Eastern mysticism in its view of God, its gloomy view of the material world, and the hope that death will bring one to a higher level of consciousness.

We don't need to imagine, as some New Age gurus do, that Jesus traveled to India to learn all this; these were popular ideas around the Mediterranean. A cynic once described war as "God's way of teaching Americans geography." The conquest of parts of India by Alexander the Great similarly made the ancient Greeks aware of "trendy" Brahmin and Buddhist thought. Reincarnation was also a live issue, one that Gnostics toyed with, warning against being "cast into another flesh" (NHL: 120).

Maybe Gnostics borrowed these ideas from India; maybe they walked the mystic path to the same terminal point. The ideas that everything is God, or within God, or pictures of God, the world is an illusion, all things are prone to change, and the dead return to new souls show up around the world, like the magic with which Gnostic writings are also laced. Mystical experiences, sometimes prompted by drugs such as monoamine serotonin, psilocybin, amanita mushrooms, or morning glory seeds, have led modern people to experience the "unity state" of consciousness.

Is that a reason to believe the "I am God" experience, or to doubt it? Drugs do not often cause people to experience the Christian God, or the Sky Father known to primitive peoples around the world. But the erasing of boundaries in the mind is often caused by meditation, drugs, or mental illness. I think that's a reason to be suspicious of it. If you can explain a mental state physically, that also explains it away. If you're hit on the head, you see stars. But unless the damage is severe indeed, you don't point a telescope at them.

## GNOSTICISM AND ISLAM

Mohammed, like Valentinus and Mani, borrowed religious

ideas from all directions. Maybe Gnosticism was one of his sources.

Allah is not as remote as the Gnostic God; he created the heavens and earth, sends messengers, protects the faithful, and punishes unbelievers. But compared to how Jesus spoke of his Father, Allah still seems a long ways off. Mohammed also felt it dishonored this pure God, who did not get his hands dirty in the world, to say so great a prophet as Jesus died on the cross. Many Muslims still believe the "stunt double" theory of the crucifixion.

Some Gnostic texts speak of the Father, the Mother, and the Son. Perhaps it was that kind of theology that led Mohammed to think that the Christian Trinity consisted of Father (God), Mother (Mary), and Son (Jesus). The third-century Gnostic Mani founded a world religion with branch offices in Arabia. Some have suggested that Mohammed borrowed ideas about Jesus from that bank.

## GNOSTIC TEXTS AS A RESPONSE

It seems then that Gnostic thought resembled Hinduism, Buddhism, Greek polytheism, Platonism, and even, at times, Islam far more than Christianity or Judaism. Given that Gnostics cared so little about what Jesus actually said, why did they talk about him so much? Why didn't they put Gnostic theology in the mouth of Plato, Pythagoras, or Krishna instead?

Michael Jordan is famous for sky-high leaps, which is why he was asked to endorse shoes. If your product is heaven, who better to endorse it than Jesus Christ?

Gnosticism can be seen as a pagan response to the Jewish and Christian challenge. It is as if Gnostics were saying, "You claim there is only one God and our gods are untrue. Hera and Zeus may indeed have been a bit clownish at times—our own critics say the same. All right, they were lower-order angels. Don't laugh!

Watch what happens when we demote your 'Only True Creator God' as well!"

In *On the Origin of the World,* the chief archon created seven androgynous god-children. He formed heavens for them, and said, "It is I who am God, and there is no other one that exists apart from me." Saying this, the author informs us, he "sinned against all the immortal beings." He then created a "four-faced chariot" called a "cherubim," archangels, gods to rule each of the 72 languages of man, serpent-like angels, "and another being, called Jesus Christ, who resembles the savior above in the eighth heaven" (NHL: 175).

*The Apocalypse of Peter* and some Gnostic texts (not all agree) say it was this false Jesus who died on the cross:

> He whom you saw on the tree, glad and laughing, this is the living Jesus. But this one into whose hands and feet they drive the nails is his fleshly part, which is the substitute being put to shame, the one who came into being in his likeness (NHL: 377).

Jesus said, "Take up your cross and follow me." The Gnostic Jesus, by contrast, promised his disciples that like him, they could avoid suffering. "I shall be with you in order that none of your enemies may prevail over you." Pagels points out that Gnostics who denied the cross were less likely to die as martyrs.[12] They found a way to save Christ (and themselves) and put Jesus to death at the same time.

In the True Buddha temple near the Microsoft headquarters in Redmond, Washington, I found three rows of deities: dark Tibetan and Indian gods, peaceful bodhisattvas and Buddhas, Chinese gods, and an idol of the Master of the temple, the "living Buddha," Lu Shengyan. Here was "open commensality,"[13] as radical scholar John Crossan described it—free fellowship for everyone without discrimination or borders, old and new gods worshipped together, no locked doors or oceans to separate concepts of the divine. The smallest of the pack was a little statue of Jesus, looking as if he were about to be mugged by a scowling Hindu sky god.

This was the true situation in the second century.

History hung in the balance, as neo-Gnostic scholars often truthfully point out. Here issues that would change the world waited to be decided. Did the compassion of Jesus mean that the Christian church would become a platform for worship of the divine within oneself? Would Christ be torn to bits by Greek polytheism, Egyptian magic, and Indian pantheism? Does diversity mean that God must become another man-made idol? The early church decided to discriminate against gods to save humanity.

One of Jesus' most famous sayings was, "You will know them [the trees] by their fruit" (Matthew 7:20). In the following chapters we will consider how Christian and Gnostic trees are rooted in history. Then we will begin to look at the very different kinds of fruit that grow from them.

# NOTHING THE GNOSTICS SAY HAPPENED, DID

WHY WEREN'T GNOSTIC TEXTS included in the New Testament? The question is often asked in a tone of bafflement, like the question, Why couldn't Romeo hold Juliet's hand just a few more minutes before plunging the knife into his own heart? Or it's asked in a tone of suspicion, like the inquiry, Where were you on the morning of September 11? Dr. Pagels put it matter-of-factly: "Can we find any actual, historical reasons why these Gnostic writings were suppressed?"[1] She concluded that the reason they were banned was that some Gnostic divinities were female, and the orthodox disapproved of divine ladies. (As if the apostle Paul would have had no qualms if his converts worshiped male gods such as Anthropos, Apollo, or Vishnu. We will consider the common charge that the church had it in for women in a later chapter.)

But what *are* the actual, historical reasons that the Gnostic writings were left out of the Christian Bible? The answer is simple: more, it seems than some postmodern historians, the early Christians cared about actual history! They recognized that nothing the Gnostics said about Jesus really happened. Irenaeus found the Gnostic myth "abstruse and portentous," laboriously learned "by such as are in love with falsehood." Whether or not he was right about the motives, he was certainly right about the falsehood.

Now there is a danger in refuting an ancient myth with few modern defenders. (Or a modern novel with many.) You may look like Jimmy Carter in a boat fighting off a sick rabbit. If Christianity is the world's religious superpower, some may wonder, why are its defenders so worried about old myths and artsy detective novels?

One is faced with two bad choices. You can maintain a dignified silence, which some will mistake for tacit admission that the charges are true. Or you can denounce the error and sound defensive. "Christians sure are touchy, getting worked up over a novel! Don't they have a sense of humor?"

I do claim to have a sense of humor. But I'll give this rabbit a few good, stiff whacks for two reasons. First, to paraphrase Darth Vader, "Do not underestimate the power of the myth." When I first watched *The Matrix* during a break from teaching classes in Japan, I was so shattered by the images and concept of the world as a virtual-reality delusion that I immediately rewound it and watched it again—which, I think, is the *only* time I have ever done that with a movie. Whether in low-tech or hi-tech garb, a story that undermines how we see the world in elegant and powerful images will always attract converts—sometimes very intelligent ones. In one way or another, as the song goes, "everybody plays the fool."

There is no absolute standard for cooking chicken, and you can play many styles of music on one guitar. But the standard for news can only be what truly happened. Gnostic stories about Jesus are not valuable because they tell us that. They are valuable because they lie, and lie badly about Jesus. And that paradoxically helps reveal the truth.

## JESUS AT NAG HAMMADI

About two dozen Gnostic writings claim to tell us something new about Jesus.

Most often, the Lord appears to offer secret teachings or a secret book. The opening of *Thomas* is typical: "These are the secret teachings which the living Jesus spoke and which Didymas Judas Thomas wrote down" (NHL: 126). Sometimes the meeting, or book, comes to secret mountains. *The Gospel of the Egyptians,* supposedly written by Seth, Adam's son, takes place "in high mountains" that tower above the sky, where the sun cannot reach (NHL: 218).

Jesus meets the chosen disciple(s) before Passover, 555 days after the resurrection, or some time in between. He reveals hidden *gnosis* to (in various texts) James, Peter, Mary, John, *or* Judas, Peter *and* James, Thomas, Judas, Mary, *and* Matthew, all 12, or all 12 *plus* seven women.

The disciples ask questions. These are not questions you expect from Jewish fishermen. They are like setup shots in a metaphysical game of volleyball: "How are we detained in this dwelling place?" "Why do the powers fight against us?" "Lord, we would like to know the deficiency of the aeons and their pleroma" (all NHL: 434). "We want to understand the sort of garments we are to be clothed with when we depart the decay of the flesh" (NHL: 253). A few could have been asked by second-century Christians: "So how can we go and preach then, since we are not esteemed in the world?" (NHL: 205). None carries the faintest whiff of first-century Galilee.

*Apocryphon of John* poses a series of questions at once: "How was the Savior appointed? Why was he sent into this world? Who was the Father who sent him? What aeon shall we go to?" (NHL: 105). More often, questions are interspersed in an easy-to-follow question-and-answer format. In *Dialogue of the Savior,* Matthew says, "I want to see the place of life where there is no wickedness." Jesus explains that he cannot help "as long as you are carrying flesh around." Judas worries that "the governors" dwell above, and "rule over us." Jesus replies: "You will rule over them!" In chorus, the disciples inquire, "What is the fullness and what is the deficiency?" Jesus explains that the disciples themselves are the fullness, and that they "dwell in the place" where the deficiency exists—that is, the material world (NHL: 249-55).

## CUT-AND-PASTE JESUS

Bill O'Reilly often introduces his talk-show program with a dramatic outtake from a movie or speech. At the climax, when (for example) the narrator is about to name HAL, the villainous computer in *2001: A Space Odyssey,* a deep voice rumbles out, "BILLLL-OOOO-REILLY."

The Lost Gospels do much the same with Jesus. In one case, the method is particularly transparent because we have both the original Gnostic version and the altered "Christian" text. In *The Nag Hammadi Library,* translator Douglas Parrott places the two texts side by side, revealing the hands behind the curtain, so to speak (NHL: 222-43).

*Eugnostos the Blessed* is a non-Christian Gnostic text with overtones of magic, telling the story of creation, but not mentioning archons or the fall into ignorance. The title derives from *eu gnosis,* or "good knowledge."

The author begins by saying that materialists, theists, and fatalists are all wrong. The highest God is immortal, unbegotten, "unchanging good," pure reason and power, who cannot be described or known by anyone, even the gods. This ultimate God "revealed" self-begotten ones, "The Generation over Whom There Is No Kingdom among the Kingdoms That Exist." These are the prototypal humans, filled with "imperishable glory" and "ineffable joy." The Father made a man in his likeness, "Adam of the Light." The spiritual Adam and his consort, Sophia, created "Savior, Begetter of all things," also called Sophia.

Created beings then multiply like rabbits, whether by sexual union, fission, or as one cloud emerges from another: six spiritual beings, 12 powers, and 360 powers and heavens. None is ever sick or weak, but only needs to think a thing for it to come into being.

In *Sophia of Jesus Christ*, the author takes the whole kit and caboodle of this complex mythology and feeds it into the mouth of Jesus. The author offers a bit of New Testament setting first: "After he rose from the dead, his twelve disciples and seven women continued to be his followers and went to Galilee." The Savior appeared "not in his previous form, but in the invisible spirit." (Whatever it means to "appear" as an "invisible" being!) The disciples marveled, and Jesus laughed.

As in other Gnostic stories about Jesus, each disciple poses standard questions about Gnostic cosmology. Philip asks about "the underlying reality of the universe and the plan." Matthew wants to know "how was Man revealed?" Thomas asks how many aeons there are. (It turns out there are 12 in this scheme.)

The ancients did not have cut-and-paste software, but the author of *Sophia of Jesus Christ* did a creditable job. He often copies *Eugnostos* word-for-word, or with slight changes. "And the speculation has not reached the truth" became, "But the speculation has not reached the truth." "The Lord of the Universe is not rightly called 'Father' but 'Forefather'" is copied exactly, except for dropping the word *rightly*. "The Son of Man consented with Sophia, his consort, and revealed a great androgynous light" is reproduced exactly and appears after the prefix, "The perfect Savior said…"

After retelling the Gnostic myth, *Sophia* explains the evil work of the archons, led by Yaltabaoth, in detail. Jesus has come to reveal the truth about these false gods and about "the God who is above the universe," to teach the disciples to "tread upon their graves" and break their power. The disciples rejoice.

If the writer of *Eugnostos* were alive today, he would have an excellent case for a lawsuit!

## AS JESUS SAID…

Aside from inserting Gnostic speeches in the mouths of Gospel figures, some Gnostic texts borrow sayings or phrases from the New Testament. John and Paul are quoted most often. But the text copied most is that of the Beatitudes, the eight blessings Jesus gave in Matthew chapter 5 to open the Sermon on the Mount, along with the seven woes he pronounced 18 chapters later (which are paralleled in Luke 11).

The Beatitudes found in the Bible do something profound, respectful, yet revolutionary, and have gone "straight to the heart" (as Gandhi described his first reading of the Sermon on the Mount) of serious readers of every time and place:

> Blessed are the poor in spirit, for theirs is the kingdom of heaven.
>
> Blessed are those who mourn, for they shall be comforted.
>
> Blessed are the gentle, for they shall inherit the earth.
>
> Blessed are those who hunger and thirst for righteousness, for they shall be satisfied.
>
> Blessed are the merciful, for they shall receive mercy.
>
> Blessed are the pure in heart, for they shall see God.
>
> Blessed are the peacemakers, for they shall be called sons of God.
>
> Blessed are those who have been persecuted for the sake of righteousness...
>
> Blessed are you when people insult you and persecute you, and falsely say all kinds of evil against you because of Me. Rejoice and be glad...(Matthew 5:3-12).

The formula is pithy, memorable, and easily copied. (Muslims would copy it, too: "Blessed is the believer, and then again blessed, for God watches over his progeny after his death.")[3] But the true power of these sayings derives from three deeper qualities. First, each overturns our normal way of thinking, in which poverty and persecution are miserable, the squeaky wheel gets the oil, and the

300-pound defensive lineman tackles the punter. Second, six of the eight beatitudes call us to the hardest virtues—the virtues of humility, meekness, justice, mercy, making peace, and accepting blows for the sake of goodness. (Later in the sermon, Jesus introduces the phrase, "turn the other [cheek]"—Matthew 5:39.) Third, several are social virtues.

Jesus' radical social call sounds even more clearly in the woes that parallel this passage. Religious leaders are called hypocrites because they make long prayers but "devour" the homes of widows (Matthew 23:14). They tithed spices such as mint and anise, but "neglected the weightier provisions of the law: justice and mercy and faithfulness" (verse 23). They cleaned the outside of the bowl, but inside were full of "robbery and self-indulgence" (verse 25). They adorned the tombs of martyred ancestors, but were partners in shedding innocent blood (verse 27). Here, prophetic passion reveals a power that can end wars and turn playboys into saints.

The Gnostics borrowed the formula, but seldom the spirit or genius of these sayings.

*Thomas* contains seven blessings and three woes. Jesus blesses "the lion that becomes a man when consumed by a man," the poor (almost word-for-word from Matthew), those who have "suffered and found life," those persecuted by others, those persecuted "within themselves," the hungry, and the person who knows when thieves are going to break in. He curses the man eaten by a lion, Pharisees who are like a dog that keeps the cow awake and doesn't sleep himself, the "flesh that depends on the soul" and the "soul that depends on the flesh" (NHL: 126-138).

Some of these sayings are clever, which helps account for *Thomas's* popularity. I particularly like the barking dog in the barn. But none overturns conventional thinking. We know a person eaten by a lion is in trouble. By the second century, we know the Pharisees are supposed to wear black hats. None shows concern for the weak, oppressed, or hungry. (There is one possible exception:

In some translations, Jesus blesses those who are hungry because they allow someone else to eat.)

In *The Book of Thomas the Contender*, Jesus gives 43 lines of woes: "Woe to you who hope in the flesh and in the prison that will perish!…You are corrupting your souls!…Woe to you within the fire that burns in you….Woe to you because of the wheel that turns in your mind! Woe to you within the grip of the burning that is in you….Woe to you captives that are bound in caves!…Woe to you who love intimacy with womankind and polluted intercourse with them!" Then he blesses (in just six lines) those who "flee alien things," those reviled on behalf of their lord's love, and those who weep "for you will be released from every bondage" (NHL: 205-7). Here, too, Jesus affirms Gnostic convention in striking language, but shows no concern for the poor. Celibacy seems more a practical than a moral concern—it is not that certain sexual acts are wrong, but that pleasure ensnares us.

In *The Apocalypse of Peter*, Jesus offers Peter a beatitude that loses something in pithiness but gains in comprehensiveness:

> Blessed are those above belonging to the Father who revealed life to those who are from the life, through me, since I reminded [them], they who are built on what is strong, that they may hear my word and distinguish words of unrighteousness and transgression of law from unrighteousness, as being from the height of every word of this pleroma of truth, having been enlightened in good pleasure by him whom the principalities sought (NHL: 373).

Did anyone ever think such a bloated saying really came from Jesus? And if it did, would anyone have remembered it?

Jesus makes this statement in the temple. The priests don't like it (perhaps they are poets?) and rush up to stone Jesus and Peter. Jesus takes time to assure Peter that their would-be assassins are blind and without guides. He tells him to put his hands over his eyes and say what he sees. Peter complains (like Luke Skywalker), "No one can see like this!" The master tells him to try again, and this time the Force is with him: "And there came in me fear with joy, for I saw a new light greater than the light of day. Then it came down upon the Savior."

The fictional nature of the story becomes more obvious with every word. Jesus warns Peter that "the sons of this age" will "blaspheme you" because of their ignorance. This makes perfect sense in the context of the second or third centuries, when Christians such as Irenaeus ripped into Gnostic beliefs. Peter then observes the "cruci-fiction":

> I saw him seemingly being seized by them. And I said, "What do I see, O Lord, that it is you yourself whom they take, and that you are grasping me? Or who is this one, glad and laughing on the tree? And is it another one whose feet and hands they are striking?"

> The Savior said to me, "He whom you saw on the tree, glad and laughing, this is the living Jesus. But this one into whose hands and feet they drive the nails is his fleshly part, which is the substitute being put to shame, the one who came into being in his likeness" (NHL: 377).

Is *Sophia* "Christian"? Of course not. Download *The Communist Manifesto*, sprinkle in questions by John Adams, Thomas Jefferson, and James Madison, and you do not have the Bill of Rights.

Nor, obviously, is this historical. In fact, a good rule of thumb is that the more explicit and detailed the Gnostic texts are about what happened, the harder they are to believe. You can actually watch gears grind in the author's head in *The Letter of Peter to Philip*:

> Peter the apostle of Jesus Christ, to Philip our beloved brother...greetings! Now I want you to know, our brother [that] we received orders from our Lord and

the Savior of the whole world that [we] should come [together] to give instruction and preach in the salvation which was promised us by our Lord Jesus Christ (NHL: 434).

A "great light" makes the mountain glow; Jesus has arrived. Who would ask the questions the apostles then pose face to face with a glowing mountain and a man from another realm?

Lord, we would like to know the deficiency of the aeons and their pleroma...How did we come to this place... In what manner shall we depart...Why do the powers fight against us?

In response, Jesus "reads the whole lecture," as the Russians say, dictating the Gnostic catechism blow by (now) painful blow.

## HUMOR IN JUDAS

Like a Greek hero, the Gnostic Jesus shows little emotion. He does laugh occasionally, but it is a grave mistake to say, as one reader did, that this laughter makes him sound more human. He doesn't laugh when someone tells a joke about a Pharisee, a Sadducee, and a fisherman, or does an over-the-top imitation of Pontius Pilate. That might be forgivable. Nor does he laugh, as one might imagine the real Jesus doing, from joy at meeting beloved friends. What escapes the sands of Nag Hammadi is more of a cackle.

Jesus laughs once each in the four scenes of *Judas,* the most I think in any Gnostic text. In *Mary,* Peter serves as a stand-in for orthodox Christians. Here, all the disciples (who like archons sin through arrogance and are ignorant of their true position) are punching bags—except Judas.

In scene one, Jesus laughs when he finds the disciples eating a meal together, probably communion. "It is through this that your god will be praised," he remarks contemptuously. In scene two he appears again, saying he has been visiting "another great and holy generation." The disciples doubt this story, prompting the master to laugh again. "No one born of this aeon will see that generation," he states, "and no person of mortal birth can associate with it."[4]

In scene three, the disciples see a vision of people sacrificing children and wives and engaging in homosexual trysts. Jesus explains, "That is who you are. That is the god you serve." He laughs yet again when he sees a vision of the twelve stoning Judas.

In the final act, this sadistic savior (whom I would rather not give the name of Jesus) tells Judas how the wicked (the church, presumably) will "fornicate in my name and slay their children." He laughs a fourth time, prompting Judas (who is more humane) to ask for an explanation. His master replies: "I am not laughing at you but at the error of the stars, because these six stars wander about with these five combatants, and they all will be destroyed along with their creatures."

Mythology often fogs time and place (even "abolishes" time and history through ritual, said the great Mircea Eliade). The Gnostic writings are in that sense myth. But the facts Jesus reveals in his ritual appearances—Father, pleroma, aeons, Sophia, Yaldabaoth—are usually Gnosticism 101. In none of these discourses does the most mildly credible revelation about anyone living in the first century emerge.

Even bitterly anti-Christian scholars recognize that Nag Hammadi does not contain a single believable piece of new data about Jesus. This is even true of *Thomas,* the most ballyhooed Gnostic text. Sometimes you have to sift carefully to find such admissions, however.

## DOUBTING *THOMAS*

The definitive Jesus Seminar work, *The Five Gospels,*[5] seems at first, and at second and third, to loudly claim just the opposite— that *Thomas* is in some sense historically authentic. Indeed, the seminarians shout it from the mountaintop (or the title). What does "the Five Gospels" mean if not, "The Church miscounted! There are actually five Gospels, not four, and *Thomas* is at least as good as the others"? The subtitle (*The Scholar's Version*) seems to add, in a tone that some rival scholars found irritating, "We, the cream of modern scholarship, concur, and here is our decree." In case you still didn't grasp the importance of this project, the editors added a second subtitle on an inside page: "The search for the authentic words of Jesus." The stress seems to be on the word *authentic*. The point, clearly, is that it takes a great deal of research to separate truth from fiction in the Gospels, and that the search is incomplete without *Thomas*. In short, the scholars who wrote *The Five Gospels* staked their credibility squarely on the claim that *Thomas* provides a source for the words of Jesus that is as important as Matthew, Mark, Luke, and John. Neo-Gnostic scholars like Pagels and Koester often suggest that in fact *Thomas* is *more* reliable than the other Gospels. This is the point of another Jesus Seminar book, *The Q-Thomas Reader*. It is also the point of Pagels's *Beyond Belief: The Secret Gospel of Thomas*.

But all this is just a big tease. Read carefully, and you find that even the most radical skeptics realize that even the best Gnostic Gospel tells us nothing about the historical Jesus.

Seminar scholars followed a colorful procedure to evaluate Gospel sayings. After they carefully considered a phrase, each scholar dropped a bead into a voting box to indicate how closely he or she thought the saying adhered to the actual words or sentiments of Jesus. The beads came in four colors. Red (as the editors explained) meant, "That's Jesus!" Pink: "Sure sounds like Jesus." Gray: "Well, maybe." And the ominous black bead: "There's been some mistake."

Some people made fun of the system, or the presumption of those who employed it. While I have no objection to colored beads per se, I do question much of the procedure that the Jesus Seminar fellows followed, and wrote a book explaining why.[6] Yet intriguingly, in the end, even scholars as deeply invested in

*Thomas,* and in a skeptical attitude toward Christianity, found only two sayings not given in the canonical Gospels that they could claim—with a straight face—came from Jesus! Only sayings 97 and 98 were voted pink, meaning the scholars (on average) thought they sounded like Jesus:

> The [Father's] imperial rule is like a woman who was carrying a [jar] full of meal. While she was walking along a distant road, the handle of the jar broke and the meal spilled behind her along the road. She didn't know it; she hadn't noticed a problem. When she reached her house, she put the jar down and discovered it was empty.

> The Father's imperial rule is like a person who wanted to kill someone powerful. While still at home he drew his sword and thrust it into the wall to find out whether his hand would go in. Then he killed the powerful one.[7]

Both sayings are parables and speak of the kingdom of God, like the "kingdom sayings" in Matthew. Even so, the fellows had to talk themselves into buying them. They voted three times. The first two times, proponents were unable to boost the vote past the color gray. Editors of *The Five Gospels* explained some of the reasoning that appears to have swayed recalcitrant scholars. Jesus' teachings were often scandalous. Comparing heaven to a hit job is scandalous, so the second saying fit Jesus' style! (Of course the saying also fits the Gnostic attitude toward power.)

To me, both sayings sound like someone pulling a Jesus formula out of a Cracker Jack box—like the fake beatitudes that also appear in *Thomas.* Jesus is never cheaply cynical. His teachings startle, not frivolously, but deeply, and plant themselves in a healthy conscience and grow like a peach tree in warm, fertile soil. But in the parable about the basket, why does God's kingdom drain out? In Jesus' canonical parables, the kingdom grows, or is revealed as valuable. Could this be a cynical satire on the kingdom parables? If so, its meaning isn't clear enough to bite. Whatever else Jesus was, he was never an incompetent teacher.[8]

Is my objection to these sayings subjective? Perhaps. The problem with *Thomas*, and other Gnostic texts, is they never confirm themselves objectively, so you are forced to evaluate them subjectively. There are no clear internal marks of historical truth here. The Gnostics never place Jesus in a real-world setting, certainly not in first-century Palestine. The people they describe are just stick figures. They don't tell a coherent story. Nor do the Gnostics confirm one another—they can't even agree to whom Jesus gave his "secret teachings," whether he died, or whether the disciples were honest fishermen or the moral equivalent of cannibals. Despite attempts to argue for an early *Thomas*, or an early "core" to *Thomas* (talk about subjective!), most scholars agree the text was written in the second century. *Thomas* shares the general Gnostic bias against morality, placing Jesus entirely outside the Hebrew prophetic tradition of which he was actually (at least) the culminating genius. Added to all that, these sayings only mildly resemble the real words of Jesus. Put all these factors together, and the overwhelming presumption about any *Thomas* saying should be that it is *not* from Jesus.

And what if Jesus did tell these two parables? They make no difference. The point of the stories is obscure. We don't know who Jesus was talking to, where, or what about. These sayings add nothing to the picture of Jesus in the Gospels.

In effect, *The Five Gospels* makes a remarkable admission. *Thomas* is universally considered to be the most "historical" Gnostic text, which is why it, and not *Mary* or *Philip*, is the so-called fifth Gospel. The book is mentioned again and again in the writings of Jesus skeptics as a key discovery in the "search for the historical Jesus." Many claim it is more original than the canonical Gospels. Pagels yields this sledgehammer to "topple the foundations of Christianity."

But look closely, and you find that even the deconstructionists know their hammer is made out of cotton candy. Not even radical skeptics can bring themselves to say the most believable Gnostic text tells us anything new about Jesus.

Neo-Gnostic scholars know these texts are not historical, but say so in hushed tones and as seldom as possible. In her book on Mary Magdalene, Karen King admits *Mary* tells us nothing about Jesus once, in nine words: "It offers no new information about the historical Jesus."[9] *National Geographic,* announcing the discovery of the *Judas Gospel,* also allowed Craig Evans to point out that the work tells us nothing about Jesus once, in 18 pages, before Pagels buried the admission: "Well, we don't look to Gospels for historical facts, anyway."[10] This is typical. Perhaps it is not surprising if not only novelists and New Age gurus, but even respected scholars such as Harold Bloom overlook such rare disclaimers.

But the Gnostics do us a service. They show us what ancient, made-up stories about a Savior from Israel look like (and they are authored by intellectuals said to be far more clever than the writers of the canonical Gospels). If the real Gospels are (as Pagels claims) poor places to look for historical truth, then their allegedly fictional character ought to be even more obvious.

# THE GOSPELS TELL THE TRUTH ABOUT JESUS

THE GNOSTIC WRITINGS provide a "control sample" by which to test the honesty of the Gospels. Nag Hammadi mystics seldom put words in Jesus' mouth that clash with Gnostic sensibilities. (The one exception may be when Jesus blesses those who skip a meal for others.) Gnostic writers give no realistic historical details. Nor do they describe any first-century people we know from other sources. Furthermore, Gnostic texts disagree even about key facts: which disciple Jesus entrusted his secret teachings to, whether he loved or hated them, even whether he died on the cross.

Traipsing across the Gnostic mindscape in search of historical truth, we come up empty. But the exercise does turn up useful artifacts: several ways in which historical truth can be tested. Let me list eight such "criteria" by which to judge whether a story is historically true or not, as scholars who research the Gospels call them.

First, it helps if there is evidence, outside the book, of the people or places it mentions (archaeological or historical). Second, a story is more believable if (unlike the Gnostic stories) it is confirmed by more than one independent source (multiple attestation). Third, a writing written close to the time it describes is more believable than one written long after (chronology). Fourth, if things happen in one language or culture, but are written about in another, traces of original language and habits of thought make a record far more believable (cultural context). Fifth, we ask, as with the parable of the woman whose basket leaked, does a story or saying fit what we know about this person? (coherence). Sixth, there is the question of intellectual capability. Not everyone could invent a Sermon on the Mount or a parable of the good Samaritan, but almost anyone can manage a long rant about aeons, or prefix a trite epigram with the words, "The Savior said..." (genius). Seventh, an honest biographer, even if he admires his subject, will include facts that make his subject look bad. James Boswell had the highest respect for Samuel Johnson, but described Johnson's fear of death, and even (which Boswell understood less) his occasional goofiness (embarrassment). And finally, it helps if there is some difference between the way your subject talked and the way everyone else talked. Most of what Jesus says in the Nag Hammadi books fits too well with Gnostic theology. But when "Jesus sayings" stand out from both first-century Judaism and Christianity, it is particularly easy to believe Jesus really did say them (dissimilarity).

An examination of the biblical Gospels with these criteria in mind reveals that they are credible historical sources.

## EIGHT CRITERIA BY WHICH TO JUDGE TRUTHFULNESS

### Physical Evidence and History

A wealth of historical and archaeological evidence confirms that the Gospels tell about the real Jesus. Many first-rate books and Web pages discuss the issues more fully than I can here—such as, for example, the authenticity of a disputed passage about Jesus by the Jewish historian Josephus. I will skip such details so that I can concentrate on criteria that one can use while reading the Bible.

Archaeology and historical research also confirm many details mentioned by the Gospel writers, such as the titles Luke used, the sequence in which different rulers came to office, and details about early shipping both on the Sea of Galilee and the Mediterranean. Often, details or structures mentioned in the biblical Gospels yet denied by skeptics have been confirmed by archaeological digs. This includes the Pool of Siloam and the five porticoes that John mentions at the Pool of Bethesda. By themselves, such facts can't prove that everything the Gospels say about Jesus is accurate. But they do show the writers were close to the facts and were paying attention.

Most of the main events of Jesus' life, and some other facts, are mentioned by non-Christian historians within the first century: his life, profound teaching, Jewish identity, miracles, the claim that he was the Son of God, the crucifixion by Pontius Pilate, and the story that he rose from the dead. Among the non-Christian historians who mention Jesus are Josephus, Pliny the Younger, and Tacitus.

### Multiple Attestation

The Gospels agree with one another about basic facts, though they differ on details. They back up one another in intricate detail on the character of Jesus, some of his miracles, how he died, and that he came to life again. By contrast, the Gnostic texts are all over the board about the few historical claims they make—who Jesus spoke to and when, whether he loved the disciples or hated them, and which one was his favorite.

### Chronology

In the nineteenth century, some scholars argued that the biblical Gospels were not written until well into the second century, at a time when the facts had been forgotten or turned to legend. (And when the first of the Gnostic Jesus writings were produced.)

Yet the earliest extant Gospel portion—the first original copy to survive to this day—is a small passage from the Gospel of John, from about A.D. 125. That is, of course, a copy of an earlier manuscript—maybe even the original. From an archaeological perspective, this is astonishingly early. Most books of that era survive in copies that are a thousand years or more removed, at the earliest. The earliest extant Buddhist manuscript is from 600 years after the life of Buddha.

Almost every scholar now agrees that the Gospels were written in the second half of the first century. Some try to make this short gap sound as if it were actually very long—"generations" passed from the earth while the "Jesus tradition" was handed down from one person to another and garbled in the transmission. But in reality, the timespan is astonishingly short. Jesus' disciples were probably younger than he was, and could have lived long past the time the Gospels were written—along with other eyewitnesses. It is quite plausible that the apostle John wrote the main part of his Gospel—and that was the last one written. All the Gospel events, except maybe the birth narratives, were written when people who still remembered them were still alive and, probably, set to live for many more years.

### Cultural Context

Unlike the Gnostic writings, the biblical Gospels are tied to Jewish culture by numerous threads. Even the most "Christian" teachings in them echo images and ideas from deep within the collective Hebrew soul.

### Coherence

One of the remarkable untold stories of New Testament scholarship is the slow triumph of Christian evidence over skeptical dogma. A case in point is Robert Funk, founder of the Jesus Seminar. Funk was a teenage evangelist, and like Ehrman and many others, reacted angrily against that heritage when he rejected his faith. Among dogmas by which he filtered the story of Jesus, he refused to accept miracles, the resurrection, talk about the end of the world, or anything that breathed of divine authority. Of course that rules out most of the Gospels, which are the story of a Miracle and miracles.

What's amazing is that Funk and his fellow seminar scholars felt obliged to affirm so much of the story of Jesus. In part, Funk simply found many of the sayings and parables of Jesus too compelling to deny. Part of what made them compelling was what is called the "criteria of cohesion." For example, Jesus' story of the Good Samaritan fits too well with everything we know about Jesus to dismiss.

> Jesus steadily privileged those marginalized in his society—the diseased, the infirm, women, children, toll collectors, gentile suppliants, perhaps even Samaritans—precisely because they were regarded as the enemy, the outsider, the victim. The Samaritan as helper was an implausible role in the everyday world of Jesus; that is what makes the Samaritan plausible as a helper in a story told by Jesus.[1]

The Gospels reinforce one another on many subtle levels.

I mentioned earlier my study of 50 characteristics that the Gospels share in common. We've seen how the Gospels all place Jesus in a real first-century Jewish environment, relate his parables and sayings, show his respect and love toward women and other "outsiders" (the blind, tax collectors, Samaritans, lepers, the disabled)—thus puncturing just about every social barrier of his time. What becomes clear is that the Gospels are woven together not only on the surface, but by unseen threads—by evidence that, like DNA samples or fingerprints, could not have been invented.

A few of these qualities include Jesus' earthy, witty, hyperbolic style, the shocking and counter-intuitive quality of his teachings, how they speak to us on different levels, the varied but always realistic reaction of those who heard him, his social nature, how he ignored caste, how he noticed people in trees or shouting at him from the side of the road, the untidiness of the plot, the working-class character of the main characters, Jesus' emotions, and the mild, velvet touch of many of his teachings (who would invent that?) along with their unmatched, universal quality.

The story hangs together on more levels than skeptics realize. Those who refuse to see those levels—the big picture of God's redemption of humanity—like the Gnostics, have a hard time understanding how Christians have read the Bible as one book for two millennia. But that is a subject for a longer volume.

### Genius

The *Gospel of Truth* (a sermon, not a gospel) may have been written by the capable hand of Valentinus, and is rightly praised as eloquent. "For the Father is sweet and in his will is what is good. He has taken cognizance of the things that are yours that you might find rest in them" (NHL: 47).

Read the stories of Jesus interacting with people, how he healed the blind and liberated a madman on the east bank of the Sea of Galilee. Meditate on his parables, his canny but profound replies to hostile questions, the Sermon on the Mount. If I live to 100 years of age, they will always teach me.

The callow read the Gospels without being moved. We may grow used to the words, like Beethoven as elevator music, and not really hear them. Simple people (of all IQ scores) expect profound truth to be expressed in long abstract words and are disappointed when it comes in short, concrete ones. Others are what Jesus called "dull of heart"—though that can be cured—and walk past beautiful sunrises, cute babies, and great heroes with the same cynical leer.

But those who knew and spoke best were shaken and haunted by Jesus' words. Tolstoy and Gandhi were deeply touched by the Sermon on the Mount. Dickens called the parable of the prodigal son the best story in literature—and who would know better? Lin Yutang read both Eastern and Western literature and decided at the end of his life that "no one has taught like Jesus." M. Scott Peck, a fan of Freud and modern psychology who also dabbled in Buddhism, found himself shocked when he first read the Gospels— both by the authenticity with which they speak of their subject and, even more, by the character of the subject of whom they speak. He described Jesus as (among other things) the smartest man who ever lived. Such praise sounds a bit crass—like meeting an Alexander Archipelago timber wolf and saying, "Big dog!"

What lends this criteria edge is that the sayings of Jesus are not always embedded in brilliant writing. Luke is a polished and skilful classical author, but his style is very different from Jesus. And no one will invite poor Mark to teach a writers' seminar. Neither man, nor any other known Christian, could have made up Jesus. Neither could Valentinus.

### Embarrassment

Biographer A.N. Wilson wrote of John's story of Jesus meeting a woman at the well in Samaria:

> That is John's great paradox. The more he piles artifice upon artifice, trope upon trope, the more real his pictures become, to the point where it becomes almost impossible not to believe that some such conversation, with a Samaritan woman, must have taken place.[2]

Wilson is, in part, referring to the realism of this story. But he is also using another method by which scholars zero in on historical truth: the criterion of embarrassment. As I said, many of the stories in the Gospels, including this one, would have been embarrassing for Christians to write. That is another reason to believe they are accurate.

In his autobiography, Mahatma Gandhi says that when he was a lawyer in South Africa, some of his Indian clerks lived at his home. The house didn't have indoor plumbing, and they used chamber pots. Trying to rid his family of caste thinking, Gandhi asked his wife to clean the chamber pot for a new clerk, a Christian from a low caste. His wife refused. Gandhi replied, "I will not stand this nonsense in my own house." "Keep your house and let me go!" she yelled back. Mahatma ("Great Soul") Gandhi then dragged his wife to the front gate to push her into the street. "Have you no sense of shame?" she cried, tears running down her cheeks. "Where am I to go? I have no parents or relatives here to harbor me."[3]

Gandhi had a reputation for honesty, and telling this story could only enhance it. Who would make himself look like such a cad, untruthfully? Indian gurus often project a "death-like serenity" or "austere severity."[4] There is little of that in Gandhi, and none at all in Jesus.

Disciples of exalted religious teachers are even less likely to falsify bad or incriminating or even suspect incidents about their master, which is why "Jesus" gets such a pass in the Gnostic writings (as Apollonius gets a pass in his second-century biography).

The Gospels show amazing candor.

Jesus is never impassable, cool, or austere. He blesses and praises. He cries over Jerusalem. Sweat pours down his back while he prays in an olive grove. A plaintive, almost sad quality creeps into his voice: "Simon, Simon, behold Satan has demanded permission to sift you like wheat, but I have prayed for you, that your faith may not fail" (Luke 22:31-32). "Was no one found who returned to give glory to God, except this foreigner?" (Luke 17:17). "Jerusalem, Jerusalem.... How often I wanted to gather your children together, the way a hen gathers her chicks under her wings, and you were unwilling" (Matthew 23:37).

"Sinner" is one of the nicer things Jesus is called. His social status, morality, sanity, racial solidarity, tax records, and orthodoxy are all doubted. He is said to have a demon, to be insane, to blaspheme God. No Gnostic admits even the emotion of Jesus, still less that he died on the cross—"to Jews a stumbling block and to Gentiles foolishness" as Paul put it (1 Corinthians 1:23). By contrast, the Gospels contain no Teflon Savior, no "Mellow-Yellow" Jesus who saunters through life in a haze of Christ-consciousness, but a man whose reality is still shocking.

The disciples, too, are portrayed in full fumbling humanity. Scholars sometimes manage not to notice. King emphasizes the contrast between the Gnostic Mary, the "model disciple," a conduit for Jesus' secret teachings, and Peter, her "hot-headed" proto-orthodox foil.[5] Peter blusters and whines to fit, as if "hot headed" defined him as neatly as Wisdom, Life, Kingship, or Jealousy tell you all there is to know about certain aeons and archons. King writes at length about how wonderful Mary is—"It is no accident that the Savior loved her more than the others," a love "based on his sure knowledge" of this "unflinching and steadfast disciple."[6] But of course tempestuous Peter is no Gnostic invention. The canonical Gospels vividly portray his flaws—and his humanity, and the leadership Jesus gave him. What this points to is how dramatically different the canonical texts are in their frank realism. King is enthralled with her simple black hat/white hat Gnostic text and never drops a hint that the richly ambiguous canonical texts might, for a historian, offer advantages.

Meyer, too, suggests that in the Gospels, the "centrality" of Mary Magdalene is "obscured" by the interests of their authors, who "advance the cause" of male disciples, such as Peter, over her.[7] Pagels argues that John tries to undermine the Gnostics by caricaturizing "doubting Thomas" unfairly.[8]

Such suggestions betray a strange blindness.

The Gospels show the followers of Jesus in all their flaws: Mary and Martha quarreling over kitchen chores, a sinful woman falling to pieces at a party. No one takes it on the chin worse than Peter. Jesus praises him, then tells him, "Get behind me, Satan" for tempting Jesus to avoid suffering. Peter tries to walk on water, and sinks through lack of faith. He denies he ever met Jesus, then goes off by himself to cry.

One neo-Gnostic even has the gall to accuse the authors of the Gospels of doctoring the records to make the disciples sinless, then turns around and uses the very frankness of the Gospels to prove that the disciples were sinners! This is biting the hand that puts the dentures in the mouth.

In her novel about the discovery of the Nag Hammadi Library, Tucker Malarkey claimed the church fathers made the apostles "infallible" and "above sin." Four sentences earlier she wrote, "Jesus himself told [Peter] that Satan desired him, might sift him as wheat," a story preserved in Luke by those same fathers. Malarky sarcastically added, "This is the rock upon which our church is built."[9]

Indeed it is—the rock of truth. If you thought Peter was a pope, the Gospels remind you he was a fisherman!

Thomas and Mary are treated no worse.

A report comes that Lazarus is sick at his home in Judea. After carrying on ministry for a few days, Jesus says, "Let's go to Judea." The disciples remind him that he is a wanted man down there. Jesus replies, "Our friend Lazarus is asleep. I intend to go wake him." The disciples misunderstand, as usual: "Good! If he's sleeping, he must be getting better!" Jesus explains, "I mean he's dead." Thomas adds a soto voce comment: "All right! Let's go die with him!"

It is not hard to believe that the same person, when he heard reports that Jesus had risen from the dead, said, "Unless I see in His hands the imprint of the nails, and put my finger into the place of the nails...I will not believe" (John 20:25). One can always say that John made up these stories. But why shouldn't Peter, Mary, and Thomas have been the kind of people we find them described as? Nothing is more arbitrary than to dismiss a mildly embarrassing but realistic account simply because a historian can imagine dark motives for the writing of it. Besides, the Gospels treat all the disciples that way. That's one reason we can trust them. In these narratives, the future leaders of the church are not only put in an unflattering light, they are raked through the coals. It is unlikely a later Christian would have treated the "holy apostles" so harshly.

And if the disciples are being undermined by some rival—as neo-Gnostic scholars often claim—why, after they stumble, does Jesus pick them up? Why does Thomas, after all, see Christ? Why does Jesus send him to preach? (To India, tradition says.) Why is Mary the first person to see the resurrected Jesus? There is not a single scene in all the Nag Hammadi Library that portrays the disciples with such embarrassing realism.

This is risky writing. Nothing like it can be found in any of the books that are foolishly compared to the Gospels. No Jew expected the Messiah to put up with such abuse. As Peck put it, these texts often "reek of authenticity."[10]

The best explanation for the embarrassing and complex realism of these stories is that these things really happened. The people who wrote the Gospels were close to the facts and felt a heavy weight of responsibility to tell "what we have heard, what we have seen with our eyes, what we have looked at and touched" (1 John 1:1).

### Dissimilarity

Jesus not only lived a risky life, he also taught like no one else. No known Jewish teacher spoke with such sheer chutzpah, which is why he scandalized the Jewish leaders. Nor did many later Christians overstep the bounds of class and social quarantine so boldly.

To limit myself to one example, Funk pointed out that Jesus liked parties. His stories are full of celebration over a lost sheep or a lost coin, the return of a child, or a king who invites the homeless to his palace for a feast. Jesus practiced what he preached: He dined with religious leaders as well as a hodgepodge collection of blue-collar workers and sinners. His ministry began at a wedding and ended at a banquet with people he called friends.

This celebratory spirit did not come from John the Baptist, an ascetic who lived in the wilderness and dined on insects. It did not come from the Essenes, the puritanical sect that gave us the Dead Sea scrolls. It certainly didn't come from some otherworldly proto-Gnostic teacher. Nor did the later church often show such pizzazz. By standing out both from his mother culture and from the Christian movement he created, Jesus showed himself as his own person, not an invention of the later church or something they borrowed from Jewish tradition.

The Gospels are full of tidbits like that—facets of Jesus' ministry that stand out from the landscape on both sides: the term "Son of Man," the parables and aphorisms, even the quality of his miracles.

Tom Wright, who taught at both Oxford and Cambridge and is one of the greatest living New Testament scholars, has developed an even more powerful method of analyzing the Gospels that he calls "double similarity, double dissimilarity":

> When something can be seen to be credible (though perhaps deeply subversive) within first-century Judaism, and credible as the implied starting-point (though not the exact replica) of something in later Christianity, there is a strong possibility of our being in touch with the genuine history of Jesus.[11]

Wright uses this method to analyze the tale of the prodigal son. The story moves people of all cultures, but it is deeply Jewish. In it, Jesus retells the "climactic drama" of Jewish history—the restoration of Israel and the love of the Father. But from a Jewish perspective, he gets it all wrong. The time may have come, as the prophets foretold, for the sinful Gentiles, represented by the younger son, to repent and come into the kingdom of God. But the stay-at-home older brother, representing orthodox Israel, upends the national self-image—faithful, orthodox, obedient, yet somehow still wrong? The Pharisees feel the jab almost physically. And the father is "reckless, prodigal, generous to a fault," rewarding the younger son's rude demands, then abandoning dignity to run and embrace the reprobate. "Jesus is claiming to be ushering in Israel's long-awaited new world; and he is doing it, apparently, in all the wrong ways," Wright remarks.[12] The parable of the good Samaritan is recognizably Jewish; but no common Jewish teacher would have told it. The story is a bedrock of Christian hope; but is too prodigal in its love and sly in its first-century Jewish sensitivities (which changed after the fall of Jerusalem in A.D. 70) to have been invented by, say, Luke. It makes sense in the mouth of Jesus, and nowhere else.

The Gnostic writings show why it is difficult to imagine the disciples putting such words in Jesus' mouth. Greeks would have made him talk like a Greek mystic, as in Nag Hammadi. They would not know time or place well enough to make his words ring true. They might even call God the devil.

What you see in the biblical Gospels is a work of spiritual remodeling for which I cannot think of any parallels in the history of religion.

When you remodel an old house, you look for posts and bearing walls. If you develop a new variety of tomato, you have to know the optimal acidity for tomatoes, the temperature at which fruit sets, and genetics. To destroy is easier: A wrecking ball or a hoe can do the job in a moment. Nor do you need an advanced degree in architecture or aerodynamics to fly an airplane into a tower.

Jesus said, "I did not come to abolish, but to fulfill" (Matthew 5:17). And he does. Somehow, he reuses all the original materials of Judaism to remake heaven and earth. It is like building a better mousetrap with all the same materials, or reinventing the wheel while a car is driving down the Autobahn. This is a rare and powerful form of historical evidence for the historicity—and indeed divinity—of Jesus.

❖  ❖  ❖

Details can be debated, but the main facts are clear. Every evidence betrays the so-called Gospels from Egypt. No external data confirm any new claim they make. Nor do they confirm one another. They are late, distant, and un-Jewish. There is no sense of coherence between the stories they tell and anything we know about Jesus. Some sayings are clever, but much is a stale rehash of Gnostic theology. Few even threaten to shake up Gnostic theology, but fit snugly into second- or third-century Greek thought.

By contrast, while details can be debated, all sorts of strong evidence, external and especially internal, confirms the basic honesty of the Gospels. Historians and archaeologists can back up their story at many points. The Gospels also confirm one another on main points. They are our earliest records, written within the natural lifespan of Jesus' first followers. They back up one another not only about particular stories and sayings, but in subtle characteristics no one would even think to falsify, nor could. No ordinary person could have invented the stories or sayings of Jesus. No disciple would have invented what other people said about him—the fact that he couldn't do miracles in his hometown, or that he died on a cross. The Gospels honestly relate many incidents that must have been terribly embarrassing to Jesus and the leaders of the new church. They are full of precise, believable details. These details fit into one coherent, astonishing whole, and only at one time and place in history, and only in one person.

None of the evidence that confirms the Gospels comes to the aid of Gnostic texts, or of other books compared to the Gospels. I don't say this to undermine the Gnostics—that is unnecessary. But it does undermine facile chatter about how "we don't look to 'Gospels' for historical fact."[13]

But of course this does not prove every verse in the biblical Gospels is accurate. That the Gospels were written early, and mostly by Jews, does not by itself prove they told the truth. The other criteria do show that portions of the Gospels are truthful. But what about the rest? Maybe the credible parts are like nutritious raisins in an unhealthy cake. Maybe sneaky editors mixed a few truthful tidbits into a batter of politically motivated falsehood?

## THE RAISIN THEORY AND EVIDENCE FOR MIRACLES

Skeptics often fall back on the "raisin theory" of Gospel composition. In *The Five Gospels,* the Jesus Seminar color-coded one saying of Jesus, Matthew 5:44-45, by voting with beads of four different colors. "But I tell you…" (black: Jesus didn't say it) "love your enemies" (red: this he did say) "and pray for your persecutors" (gray: probably not)…God causes the sun to rise on both the bad and the good…" (pink: *sounds* like him).[14]

But shouldn't we give a historian who tells difficult facts some credit? If Gandhi told stories that put himself in a bad light, doesn't that give us reason to trust what he said about other things? He may get some facts wrong, but such stories make him basically credible. How many statements full of gutsy honesty do we need to record before we conclude, "The people who wrote the Gospels were honest men"? Especially when so many other arrows point in the same direction?

Again, my point here is not to prove that everything in the Gospels is "Gospel truth." My point is that from a historical point of view (not theological), they deserve the benefit of a lot of doubts.

What happens when you apply these criteria to stories about Jesus doing miracles? (The part of the cake skeptics most often reject.) Historian Gary Habermas has done just that.[15] He points out that the same criteria that force skeptics to admit to some of Jesus' teachings also prove many of his miracles. The miracles are attested in the earliest sources (chronology). All four Gospels describe his feeding of the 5000, the resurrection, and that he healed, cast out demons, and commanded nature (multiple attestation). The miracles fit his compassion, authority, and self-understanding, and the story the Bible tells of who he is and what he came to do (coherence). When Jesus cast out demons, he never used props as magicians do, and often he didn't even pray (dissimilarity). Gospel accounts are restrained: Unlike in the Gnostic Gospels, those whom Jesus raises from the dead do not prattle on about demons on different layers of heaven. The biblical accounts are filled with realistic circumstantial details. And many of Jesus' miracles embarrass the church. The orthodox Gospels also say it was women who saw the risen Jesus first. And to this day, some Christians prefer to think Jesus made a superior brand of Welch's grape juice.

So the raisin theory fails. The biblical Gospels as a whole show strong evidence of being true—far stronger, I would add, than ancient biographies that are generally agreed to be historical.

The Gnostic texts help confirm this. If you want to know whether you can trust the Gospels, what better than to find early "Jesus texts" known to be false to compare them to?

Nag Hammadi does not contain a single believable story about Jesus. Everything fits smoothly into the myth. The Savior does not suffer. Jesus is ineffable, unflappable, insane. No one hurls an accusation at him. He is not even served any tough first-century question about paying taxes to pagan occupiers or where Samaritans should worship. The disciples read tamely from the script, like North Korean journalists interviewing Kim Il Sun. Questions point directly to correct conclusions.

I have been looking for ancient fiction like the Gospels. Time after time—Hanina ben Dosa, Honi the Circle Drawer, Apollonius of Tyana—the volume of smoke (and hot air) proves inversely proportional to the heat.

The latest finds have captivated skeptics for 50 years. Excitement bubbles up in novels, major news journals, the Discovery Channel, PBS. In the end, as in the first century, reality "left clicks" the words, "No one has spoken like this man," underlines them, put them in bold, and writes them across history in a font normally reserved for the unexpected outbreak of peace.

# 8

# JESUS WAS THE "ORIGINAL FEMINIST"

WORDS, LIKE SPELLS, bewitch nations. While launching a revolution that would kill millions and establish a God-hating totalitarian state, Vladimir Lenin wrote about democracy, peace, and even salvation. "Soviet power offers immediate *democratic peace* to all peoples and an immediate armistice on all fronts," he wrote in a tract dated October 25, 1917, the day his troops seized power in Russia by force. A movement eventually reveals itself for what it is. But often you need to sidestep an initial barrage of propaganda to see the truth.

One of the most popular lies of our age is that Christianity is bad for sexual progress, for the female sex in particular. The nineteenth-century women's movement included pious, progressive women such as Harriet Beecher Stowe. But for some time, Christianity has been seen as an enemy of sexual progress. In the 1920s, Margaret Mead wrote a tale of the South Pacific, *Coming of Age in Samoa*, which pictured free and easy bisexual "love under the palms"[1] and established her as the "mother goddess" of anthropology. To the Aquarian generation, "free love" and "equal rights" seemed to go together. *The Humanist Manifesto II*, written in 1973, the year abortion was legalized, complained that orthodox religions often help "unduly repress sexual conduct."

*The Da Vinci Code* also accused the church of repression and sexism. Jesus himself was the "original feminist." Dan Brown quoted *Mary* and *Philip*, which portray Mary Magdalene as (at least) Jesus' most competent and enlightened follower. In *Mary*, Levi says Jesus "loved her more than us." *Philip* portrays her as his "companion" (or, said Brown, wife), whom he used to "kiss frequently on the mouth." The early church practiced ritual sex, Brown suggested, and women acted as leaders and apostles. But then "powerful men" used the orthodox Gospels to "put women in their place." Females were portrayed as accomplices of the devil, and natural love (under the mistletoe rather than the palms) became a shameful act (the church is still blushing). Having "demonized" female spirituality, mass murder followed. The church (said Brown) committed a holocaust against the most intelligent women, burning *five million* to death as witches— "female scholars, priestesses, gypsies, mystics, nature lovers, herb gatherers."[2]

Neo-Gnostic scholars admit Brown cut a few corners with his facts. *Philip* doesn't quite say Jesus kissed Mary "on the mouth"— there is a hole in the manuscript. "Companion" did not really mean "wife" in the "original Aramaic"—and anyway, the book was written in Greek, and translated into Coptic. Brown's count of witches burnt was a hundred times too high. A quarter of the victims were male, and accusations were more often made by village women than the church.

But neo-Gnostic scholars save as much of the story—contrasting liberated Gnostic sexuality and Christian "repression"—as possible. While Christians worshiped a Father in heaven, goddesses such as Sophia, Zoe, and Norea play lead roles in Gnostic mythology. These divinities even rebuked the Hebrew God, as Pagels pointed out. In some forms of Gnosticism, the ultimate God was a male-female pair. While Jesus was, no doubt, extraordinarily respectful towards women (Tucker Malarkey supposes he picked this up in Egypt, where the goddess Isis was worshiped), it is often said the church put an end to that. Pagels pointed out that Tertullian expressed "outrage" over "heretical women" who dared to teach, argue, even baptize.[3] But orthodoxy won, and as Malarkey dramatically put it, "half of humanity was obscured from view."[4]

The role Mary Magdalene plays in Gnostic texts is central to this story. In the Gospel named for her, Mary is Jesus' wisest apostle and confidante. If the two were a couple (Marvin Meyer also toys with this idea), perhaps that would help the church get over its fear of girls.

But the truth about Christianity and sex, I will argue in this and the following chapter, differs dramatically from this caricature. Dan Brown was right on one point: It would be fair to call Jesus the "original feminist." But while Gnostics made Mary (like Jesus) a mouthpiece for their ideas, in general, their faith had little use for sex or women. And despite many false starts, the Christian Gospel has helped women even in non-Christian countries more than anything else.

First, in all four Gospels, Jesus loved and challenged women in a way that astounded the ancient world and still shocks those who read carefully. New Testament scholar Walter Wink noted that in "every single encounter," Jesus "violated the mores of his kind" for interacting with women.[5] Let's look closely at four of those meetings.

## JESUS AND WOMEN

### Encounter One: To Stone or Not to Stone?

Half a century after Jesus, the Greek sage Apollonius is said to have traveled the world from India to Africa. One day he arrived in the city of Ephesus (now in modern-day Turkey), where a plague was raging. "Help us!" leading men of the city asked. "What can we do to stop this plague?" Apollonius looked around and noticed a beggar. "That beggar is not human!" He told them. "He is a monster in human form. Stone him to death, and the plague will cease!" The townspeople hesitated, but the sage insisted. Finally, they obeyed. As the beggar died, his eyes began to glow, revealing his monstrous character and justifying the sage's diagnosis.

Anthropologist Rene Girard argues that behind this account lies a genuine event. He notes that in times of crisis, when a country is invaded, crops fail, or an epidemic breaks out, a community often looks for a scapegoat: someone untowardly handsome or ugly, an outsider, beggar, or crone, and focuses its wrath on him. But that first stone does not leave the fist easily! Something in us protests against attacking a defenseless person, whatever we have accused him or her of. Apollonius thus played a useful catalytic role: helping a crowd, eager for blood, overcome its humanity. Girard thinks a beggar did die in Ephesus. But what about the glowing eyes? Simple. The crowd put a postmortem mythological spin on the incident to cover up or justify its crime.[6]

Jesus once dealt with a crowd in the same mood. The story is told in John 8. A woman was found in the wrong bed. As still seems the norm in northern Nigeria and rural Pakistan, the man escaped. Dragging the woman along, someone suddenly hit on a brilliant idea: Let's see how the famous rabbi deals with her! Yes! They could kill two birds with one stone, so to speak. All his namby-pamby talk about turning the other cheek, his infuriating mask of piety and the sophistry with which he defended healing on the Sabbath—what will he do when the law unambiguously demands punishment? Blood sport was popular in the Roman world, but baiting a holy man is always brilliant game.

And so they dragged the young lady to Jesus. "Will you uphold the law, rabbi? Or are you going to 'have mercy' on this sinner and betray the sacred teachings of our people? Not forgetting that our traditions are daily under assault by the Roman occupiers."

Jesus doodled on the ground for a moment. Was he thinking? Tracing the sixth commandment with a rock? Biding for time? Finally he pulled himself up and said the last thing anyone expected. "All right—go ahead and stone her." And then he added, "Just one thing: Let someone who has never sinned toss that first missile."

To Hebrews, a claim to sinlessness would not just be arrogant, it would be blasphemy. So while Apollonius tore down the barriers to murder, Jesus raised them far higher, and laid barbed wire and shards of glass on top. One by one, the "righteous" dropped their stones and slunk away. "Neither do I accuse you," Jesus told the woman he had saved.

Just before she walked off, Jesus added a few words to enrage us as well: "Go and sin no more."

### Encounter Two: Can We Talk?

When I was a boy, I lived in Alaska. The pastor of the church my family attended was known to visit Juneau's popular saloons. He didn't go to drink; he went to talk missing husbands home. But a preacher has to watch his reputation. Juneau was a small town, and we were not a fellowship that put wine in the communion cups.

Jesus took an even greater risk when he spoke with a woman beside a well in Samaria. A man did not talk alone with a strange woman. It was an especially embarrassing encounter because this woman had had five husbands, and the one whom she was living with at the time was not her husband (John 4:18). Furthermore, this was a time when neighboring villages might speak different languages, wear different clothes, and wage war on one another. (Not that the West Bank has changed that much!) This lady was a Samaritan, a Capulet to the Montagues, a Crip to the Bloods. The Samaritans were hated half-breeds known for slipshod adherence to a bastardized form of Judaism.

Jesus did not seem to mind.

"Give me a drink."

The woman, startled, stared at him. She tried irony. "How is it that You, being a Jew, ask me for a drink since I am a Samaritan woman?"

"If you knew the gift of God, and who it is who says to you, 'Give me a drink,' you would have asked Him, and He would have given you living water."

"Oh?" She must have smiled, noting the bait but not taking it. "You have nothing to draw with and the well is deep; where then do You get that living water?"

Bit by bit, Jesus drew this stranger out, probing her emotional wounds gently but firmly, like a doctor. ("You have had five husbands, and the one whom you now have is not your husband.") To him, she was not just a Samaritan, a woman, or even a sinner. He met her soul to soul. He affirmed purity again, but moved beyond it. Neither slave to sex nor slave to fear of it, this Jesus truly was "unsponsored and free," as Harold Bloom described the sage of *Thomas*.[7] He not only gave this triple outcast living water, he made her the center of God's plan for her town. Dropping her pitcher, she ran home and shouted, "Come, see a man who told me all the things that I have done; this is not the Christ, is it?" (John 4:29).

### Encounter Three: Jesus and the Party-Crasher

If a respected pastor attends your barbecue, you probably know what to expect: socializing, a few preacher jokes, perhaps a bit of lounge-chair theology. You do not expect a shady young woman to crash the party, fall on the ground crying, pour perfume on the preacher's feet, then clean them with her hair!

This happened to Jesus. The host, a religious leader named Simon, was naturally shocked. He was even more shocked at how Jesus reacted. He didn't ask the girl to make an appointment with Peter for counseling during office hours. He didn't edge his couch away in fear of what people would say, or of being polluted by whatever madness possessed her. He didn't even apologize on her behalf. He just sat. Simon thought to himself, "If this man were a prophet, He would know who and what sort of person this woman is who is touching Him, that she is a sinner" (Luke 7:39).

Jesus then told his host a tale of two debtors. One owed his creditor a huge sum, the other a small one. Knowing neither could pay, the creditor canceled both debts. "Which of them," Jesus asked, "will love him more?" Simon replied, "I suppose the one whom he forgave more." "You have judged correctly," Jesus answered. "Do you see this woman? I entered your house; you gave Me no water for My feet, but she has wet My feet with her tears and wiped them with her hair. You gave Me no kiss; but she, since the time I came in, has not ceased to kiss My feet...I say to you, her sins, which are many, have been forgiven, for she loved much."

In a similar incident at the home of Lazarus, Martha, and Mary, the latter anointed Jesus with nard, a precious spice from the foothills of the Himalayas. Judas complained that the perfume could have been sold for a fortune for charity. Jesus responded, "Let her alone, so that she may keep it for the day of My burial. For you always have the poor with you; but you do not always have Me" (John 12:7-8).

The Hollywood version of such a story would involve sexual banter. Jesus was a young man, after all. (Mary might have been a white-haired cookie-baking friend of his mother, for all we know, but she is always pictured as young.) In the evangelical version, Mary would contribute the funds to Compassion International. But Jesus looked beyond sex, money, and even sin, to love women, respecting the humility, faith, and love behind their economic choices.

### *Encounter Four: Do Women Belong on Campus?*

The Gospels also relate a more mundane dialogue at the same home—a dialogue that would have far-reaching implications.

Martha was outside, preparing a meal. She had the flat bread all cooked. But a fish stew, with a *tilapia* from the Galilean co-op carefully spiced with garlic and onions, was brewing, and with melons to cut, wine to serve, and 15 guests lounging around, her hands were full. Where was that Mary? Inside, leaning against the table, interrupting the men in their theological arguments with pert questions. Mary was letting Martha do all the work! Martha tapped Jesus on the shoulder, sure that with stomachs rumbling, he would understand where his interests lay. "Jesus! Tell Mary to come help! She's just sitting around while I have to do everything!"

If the authors of the Gospels wanted (as neo-Gnostic scholars insist) to downgrade the feminine, here was their golden opportunity. Jesus would surely reply: "Right. Look, Mary! The kingdom of God is for gentlemen. The disciples are all men—haven't you noticed? Eve sinned first, remember? Get outside and help cook! Hey Martha! More bagels!"

Instead, Jesus replied, "Martha, Martha. You are worried and bothered about so many things; but only one thing is necessary, for Mary has chosen the good part, which shall not be taken from her" (Luke 10:41-42).

What does that mean? In practice, it meant the first schools for girls in India, Japan, and China. How can a Christian deny young women what Christ himself called "the better part"?

The message to Martha, while harder to swallow, is equally loving, with the unsentimental earthiness of the biblical Gospels. "Thanks, friend, for the eats. But don't try to manipulate me, and don't ask me to manipulate your sister into settling for second best."

The Gospels are full of such dignity-enhancing encounters,

in which you can hear tectonic plates rumble. Jesus rebukes his mother, then listens to her plea to liven up—I was going to say booze up—a wedding party. (So weddings are sacred! And God does listen to prayer!) He heals a woman who touches him in a crowd. (So we are not made unclean by disease, but can bring the sick cleanliness?) Reluctantly, it seems—or is that a twinkle in his eye?—he grants a foreign woman's request to heal her daughter. He mourns for pregnant women, even with a cross on his back. He thinks of his mother while dying.

Esther A. De Boer points out that even Jesus' stories refer to female experiences—the pain of giving birth, handling leaven and salt, and keeping house—as well as male experiences such as shepherding, fishing, and farming.[7]

Jesus was indeed the original feminist. He was not sentimental about the fair sex in the Victorian manner. He looked women in the eye and called for purity and sacrificial love.

The respect with which Jesus treated Mary did catch the Gnostic eye. I will show in the next chapter that his example also influenced people of other religions. But Gnosticism was not, at heart, friendly to romantic love, or women.

## GNOSTICISM AND SEX

Sex plays cosmic, historical, and practical roles in Gnosticism: each convoluted, some obscene, and few cheerful. While there is a great deal of confusion over whether divine beings are sexual or asexual, what lay with what to produce whom, and whether or not marriage is permissible, two facts emerge clearly from these texts: Sex is bad, and the female sex is worse.

In the beginning was the Father, the One. Some Gnostics say there were two: the Doad, or male-female pair. The origin of the aeons is sometimes described in graphic, sexual detail, the universe appearing from monstrous sexual organs. At other times creation seems asexual, like a paramecium splitting in two.

It is unclear whether sex or matter comes first. In *The Sophia of Jesus Christ*, Sophia is a "divine consort" but engages in "unclean rubbing" with the archons (NHL: 235). In *Hypostasis of the Archons*, the chief archon plots with "authorities" and has them commit adultery with Sophia. Some say they try to rape her, but she escapes ("beings that merely possess a soul cannot lay hold of those that possess a spirit") and turns into a tree. She laughs at their "witlessness" and "blindness," but they rape and abuse her "shadowy reflection" (NHL: 164). Through such unions come forth "the last of the changeable bonds" and "every sin and injustice and blasphemy and the chain of forgetfulness and ignorance."

*Apocryphon of John* says the chief archon raped or seduced Eve, and she bore Cain and Abel. The author concludes: "Now up to the present day sexual intercourse continued due to the chief archon. And he planted sexual desire in her who belongs to Adam. And he produced through intercourse the copies of the bodies, and he inspired them with his counterfeit spirit" (NHL: 119).

Adam and Eve also "erred ignorantly like beasts." In *On the Origin of the World*, evil archons rejoice to see them having sex, thus bringing more children into this deluded world. In *Thomas the Contender*, Jesus asks Thomas how a body that derives from intercourse can beget anything more than an animal that "changes and decays." He warns against the "fire" that burns in bodies, making minds "drunk" and souls "deranged." Those who seek truth will make wings to fly from "the lust that scorches the spirits of men" (NHL: 202-3).

*The Authoritative Teaching* agrees. When the spirit "was cast into the body," it became "brother to lust and hatred and envy." Wine is the "debaucher." The soul forgets "brothers" and "father," "for pleasure and sweet profits deceive her." Mankind is "bound in nets of flesh." The text offers a vivid metaphor of how the archon catches people like fish in a dragnet or on a line. The net "sucks us" into its mouth, while water "flows over us, striking our face." Submerged in the "filthy mud" of material existence, under fathoms of water, "man-eaters" come to "seize us and swallow us," rejoicing (here the metaphor passes from commercial to sports fishing), "for by the ruse of food he brought the fish up on a hook."

What sort of food does "the Adversary" use as bait? Nice clothes, money, vanity, envy, and most of all, "ignorance and ease." The worthy soul realizes these are "transitory," and "despises life." She strips off "this world, while her true garment clothes her within" (NHL: 306-10).

*Exegesis on the Soul* tells the Gnostic story of the soul from the fall to her return to heaven. The soul is female, but androgynous in her original form. She "fell down into a body," and was used and abused, raped and bought as a prostitute by "wanton creatures" who passed by (NHL: 192).

The author borrows the analogy from Hebrew Scripture. In the biblical version, the girl who prostitutes herself is Israel worshiping false gods. A woman should be faithful to her husband, and the soul to God, who made her. The Gnostic writer quotes the poetic cries of Jeremiah, Hosea, and Ezekiel, but changes the meaning of the analogy. Now material existence itself is defiling. "But what does 'the sons of Egypt, men of great flesh,' mean if not the domain of the flesh and the perceptible realm and the affairs of earth…?" The goal of life is for the soul to escape the "treachery of Aphrodite" and "ascend to her perfect husband."

The author probably would have agreed with Buddha, who upbraided a disciple for making love to his wife: "It is better for you, foolish man, that your male organ should enter the mouth of a terrible and poisonous snake, than it should enter a woman."

Only so glib and egocentric an era as ours could turn these folk into characters from *Sex in the City,* spouting the philosophy that sex is natural and nothing to be ashamed of. Nag Hammadi admits, in a way, that sex comes from "God." But this "God" is an archon, plotting to use sex like Sauron's ring "to rule them all and in the darkness bind them."

Romance, or making love, are just not Gnostic concepts. Some

Gnostics married, however. *Philip* says the "holy of holies is the bridal chamber." Christ came to "repair the separation" between male and female, and part of that reunion, he tells us, occurs in the marriage bed.

*The Testimony of Truth*, however, says "the law" (presumably Jewish law) commands marriage, so mortals will "multiply like the sand of the sea." But passion "constrains" and "defiles" those begotten in our sorry realm. The Jordan River is an image of sensuality, with John the Baptist as "archon of the womb." The writer rebukes people who have sex and who are "gratified by unrighteous Mammon," since the same evil archon is father of both money and sexual desire (NHL: 450-57).

No wonder that sect died out!

## GNOSTIC LIBERTINES?

Some Gnostics were accused, on the other hand, of wild carousing. Clement of Alexandria said followers of Carpocrates, who taught in the same city, held wives in common and practiced orgies under the guise of love feasts. Hippolytus claimed he was approached by female followers of Valentinus for sex. Irenaeus said that for Gnostics, "it is impossible that spiritual substance (by which they mean themselves) should ever come under the power of corruption." So some went to gladiator games, others ate at pagan feasts, and some "are in the habit of defiling those women they have taught the above doctrine." Many such women confessed when they returned to "the church of God."

We are sometimes told, "Now that Gnostics can speak for themselves, we realize the orthodox heresy hunters were deceiving us with these lurid tales. There's nothing about free love in the Nag Hammadi texts! In fact, many of these people believed in abstinence!"

Having met some abusive gurus and researched others, I am not so sure. Some gurus set forth elaborate metaphysical systems to justify free sex, at least for leaders (who get first pick of women). The obsession with cosmic sex that is found in the Gnostic literature might easily make for the kind of pickup lines you hear in such sects: "I perceive that you are the incarnation of Sophia. I just happen to be the incarnation of her consort. Too bad your husband is such an unenlightened oaf." The "bridal chamber" in *Philip* may be like euphemisms to "consort practice" that Asian tantrics use. But that's just speculation. What's certain is that asceticism is often the doppelganger of a predatory sexuality, and need not be mutually exclusive.

## GNOSTICISM AND FEMALE INFERIORITY

Many Gnostics assumed, with most Greek philosophers, that women were inferior, perhaps not quite human. *The Tripartite Tractate* says, "He became weak like a female nature" (NHL: 73), and speaks of "the illness which is femaleness" (NHL: 82). *Sophia of Jesus Christ* also mentions "the defect in the female" (NHL: 236). *(First) Apocalypse of James* says that "the perishable has [gone up] to the imperishable and the female element has attained to this male element" (NHL: 267). *Zostrianus* warns us to "flee from the madness and the bondage of femaleness and choose for yourself the salvation of maleness" (NHL: 430).

Joseph Smith promised American Indians they would become "white and delightsome" if they converted to Mormonism (2 Nephi 30:6). *Thomas* offers a similar ray of hope to those guilty of double X chromosomes:

> Simon Peter said to them, "Let Mary leave us, for women are not worthy of life." Jesus said, "I myself shall lead her in order to make her male, so that she too may become a living spirit resembling you males. For every woman who will make herself male will enter the kingdom of heaven" (NHL: 138).

Some scholars argue this passage was tacked on after the rest of the text was written. Maybe so—*Thomas* is a stack of unsorted goods, put together Yaltabaoth knows by whom or when. But an earlier saying in *Thomas* also suggests salvation through gender confusion:

> When you make the two into one, and when you make the inner like the outer and the outer like the inner, and the upper like the lower, and when you make male and female into a single one, so that the male will not be male nor the female be female...then you will enter [the kingdom] (NHL: 129).

My point is not that modern hedonistic America is right, and the Gnostics and early Buddhists wrong. The playboy lifestyle is also deeply demented and has hurt millions of children. Our culture strip-mines the body in the same way the Gnostics strip-mined the soul. Like a bear, or vein of uranium ore, sex is powerful, and needs restraint. Like wild flowers or a tourmaline crystal, sex is also beautiful, and begs protection. Fools rush in where wise lovers fear to tread, not because they are more virile, but because they are too stupid to see what they are stomping on. In the end, unrestrained lust not only messes up lives, but spoils romance and even pleasure. The party animal becomes just another tame beast strutting among the herd, blind to beauty.

But the "spiritual" view of sex is also less than human. Some Buddhists keep themselves "pure" by picturing feces and decay. It is not surprising that despite the talk about the "treachery of Aphrodite," some Gnostics were also accused of orgies. The south wind of sensuality and the north wind of contempt create a vortex that tears romantic love apart.

It's an old story: "Can't live with 'em, can't live without 'em." Can the Gospel as proclaimed in the Bible help us find the secret to sexual love?

9

# THE GOSPEL BRINGS
# TRUE SEXUAL LIBERATION

OFTEN THE FACT that the church has it in for women is so deeply assumed that people are surprised if anyone denies it. "How often do women serve as priests or bishops?" we are asked. "How many matriarchs have you seen in the back of the Popemobile?"

Like everyone else, my views have been shaped (or warped) by my experiences, and this is especially true when it comes to sex, power, and religion. I'll begin by telling my story. Then I'll introduce broader recent data about the status of women around the world that I think supports my prejudice and disproves the myth. Finally, I'll fill the gap between ancient and modern experience by showing how women came to enjoy greater freedom, and the role Jesus' life and teachings play in helping us treating both genders respectfully.

## WHERE WHORES COME FROM

After attending a discipleship training school in Hong Kong in 1984, I traveled south and west with 17 other young Christians from different countries to preach the gospel. Our first stop was Thailand. Our guide, a dynamic long-term missionary, led us to tribal villages to put on open air meetings. Along the way he told us wild stories about Burmese jets bombing jungle villages then disappearing, and a free-for-all between warlords for opium, gems, and Thailand's open sex trade. The girls were not volunteers. Sometimes they were chained to beds and burned to death in brothel fires.

We stopped in a village of the Lisu tribe. As we turned off the reddish dirt road toward a cluster of bamboo huts, pretty young girls with colorful tribal uniforms and shy smiles were playing a game with a chestnut-like object on the ground. Our guide told us the year before he had brought another team to stay the night in that village. The women were put in one hut, the men in another. The men were asked, "Would you like a girl for the night?" The going rate in these hills, the missionary told us, was a dollar a night for one girl.

We set up in front of a bamboo hut facing our *de facto* parking lot to perform a drama about Jesus. I'm no good as an actor, so I wandered behind the hut to "offer prayer support."

I am not a Pentecostal. Nor, at the time, did I relate well to teenage girls—the scars from my own teenage years were too fresh! But as I prayed, I found myself crying. A picture of mixed words and images came to my mind, which I can put in these words: "God loved the world and sent his Son to save it. This village is also a world. A child of God must come here, too, to live and maybe give his life, to save these people."

Twice more in my early years as a missionary—on the east coast of Taiwan outside the home of a girl sold into prostitution, and in a dream before a research trip in Southwest China—I had similar experiences. I concluded that the thing for me to do was help girls sold into sexual slavery. For several years I tried to do that: researching, preaching in villages, writing letters, writing a series of exposé articles, and trying to help the girls themselves.

Ambassador John R. Miller, point man for combating human trafficking in the George W. Bush administration, said that probably more than half of the agencies that combat the sex trade are religious.[1] While there are few Christians in Thailand, Taiwan, or Japan, I found that many or most of the people sticking up for women in the sex trade were believers. Why do Christians meddle with such poor Sunday school prospects?

I believe God had revealed his burning love to me directly. I may have been prepared to hear that message by the example of missionaries I met—our group was passionate about "mercy ministries," and about Jesus, who also meddled.

Also, that year I was meditating on the book of Isaiah. Twenty-two years later, I still have the Bible I used (a New American Standard Bible given to me by a young Norwegian roommate because I hadn't brought my own). Passages are underlined, sometimes with notes in the margins. Isaiah 42:22 was one passage I underlined: "This is a people plundered and despoiled; all of them trapped in caves, or are hidden away in prisons; they have become a prey with none to deliver them, and a spoil, with none to say, 'Give them back!'" I underlined Isaiah 52:7 in red: "How lovely on the mountains are the feet of him who brings good news, who announces peace and brings good news of happiness...." Then I wrote in the upper margin, "After idea of going to hill tribes...." I also underlined the famous Isaiah 61 passage that Jesus read in Nazareth. "The LORD has anointed me to bring good news to the afflicted; He has sent me to bind up the brokenhearted, to proclaim liberty to captives and freedom to prisoners" (verse 1).

So I was prepared to help the oppressed and victims of the sex trade by the God of the Old Testament, whom Gnostics dismiss with contempt. And of course, the Old Testament was interpreted in the light of Jesus.

This is why, to me, the gender gap behind the pulpit seems a trivial gauge of this world's broken relationships.

My visits to pray and learn in Snake Alley, the red-light district in Taipei where I coined the term "assembly line prostitution," also explain why the issue of whether God is described with male or female symbolism leaves me just as cold. The principle deity in the largest temple was a female Guan Yin, the "goddess of mercy." Her temple had been built before John Hancock signed his name to the Declaration of Independence, but she did not seem to impede the flow of 14-year-old girls from scenic mountain villages to this hell-hole. Likewise, Kali is one of the most popular deities in India, one of the few countries in the world where women die younger than men. Worshipping female divinities and kindness to mortal women seem to be two separate issues.

I also came to another conclusion that year. Reform seldom moves from the top down. Nor does it come from the bottom up. Social reform moves inside out, then trickles up. I didn't care much about teenage girls, but God gave me holy passion for these children, and I got the idea he wanted me to do something for them.

So that is my personal testimony. Is it just an anomaly, or does it relate to a broader pattern of human experience? I believe objective data do in fact suggest that the gospel is what liberates women most.

## RELIGION AND THE STATUS OF WOMEN AROUND THE WORLD

In 1988, the United Nations Population Crisis Committee studied the status of women in 99 countries. Each was ranked for health, education, employment, social equality, and marriage and childbearing, according to matters such as the percentage of girls in school, death rates, and differences between the literacy rates of men and women.

The authors interpreted the results economically. Women led harder lives in poor countries, they pointed out. This was no great shock: Some of the indexes they used, such as life expectancy, clearly favored the wealthy. Neither in the study, nor in the news report that drew my attention to it, did I find any attempt to relate the status of women to religious heritage.

But there seemed to be a link. The top 26 countries all had a Christian background. The ten countries where women had the lowest status were all Muslim. Nor were all these countries poor: Oil-rich Saudi Arabia was seventh from the bottom. Japan, despite its great wealth, was only number 34, while China was in the middle at 51. India and Nepal, both Hindu countries, ranked numbers 76 and 86 out of 99.

In a dissenting article, scholar Yasmeen Mohiuddin argued that the study was unfair to Muslim countries. Among other things, it should have taken divorce into account: In some western countries, family breakup puts a great burden on women. Reworking the data provided by the United Nations, she created an alternative ranking in which the status of women was highest in the USSR, followed by Romania (one year before both collapsed).[2]

I believe Mohiuddin has a good point about families, but as a student of communism, I am skeptical of Soviet data. (What advantage did most women gain from having seats reserved for a few of them in a rubber-stamp parliament?) Even so, all 19 countries that ranked lowest in her reworked study were Muslim or Hindu. Eighteen out of 20 with the highest rankings had a Christian background, including relatively poor countries such as Poland and Jamaica.

These statistics may not, by themselves, prove the church helps women, though that is the most obvious explanation. They do make it extremely hard to claim that Christianity has been quite the force for patriarchal villainy that neo-Gnostics make it out to be.

Look closely at the history of reform, and the connection becomes clear. The gospel is like a great river flowing into a delta, branching and bringing sustenance to field after field. People often make the mistake of looking at the patchwork flow of rivulets at the mouth of the delta—the women's liberation movement from the nineteenth century, or the 1960s, rather than upstream to the source.

## JESUS AND FEMINIST REFORM

The story begins, as we saw, with the life of Jesus.

The West became Christian partly because believers sometimes followed Jesus' example. Christian women married later and had more choice in marriage than other Roman women. The church discouraged abortion (a dangerous procedure in those days) and infanticide, which was usually carried out against girls. As a result, within the Christian community, the number of women in proportion to men began to climb.[3] (The same has happened in parts of India, where Christian girls are far more likely to survive abortion than girls in other religious communities.[4]) Most early Christians were female not because Roman women were too foolish to avoid such a sexist institution, but for two reasons: girls were not killed, and Christian women had a far higher status, so more women joined.[5]

One sign that the biblical Gospels taught early Christians to respect women can be found in the writing of St. Jerome. In a biography of the "holy woman" Marcella, Jerome confessed that non-Christian readers might "smile to find me lingering over the praises of weak women." In response, he pointed out that women supported Jesus' ministry and watched over him at the cross. Furthermore, Mary Magdalene, "called 'of the tower' because of her earnestness and ardent faith," met the risen Christ before the male apostles. So those who looked down their noses at women should ponder their "pride." Virtue should be judged "not by the sex but by the mind" (Epistle 127).

Like a sixth-grade boy, Jerome seemed embarrassed to say anything too nice about girls, but he realized there might be something to them. Dutch scholar Esther De Boer called Jerome's words "revolutionary," given his prejudices, and the "dualistic view of male and female in antiquity." She concluded that the Gospels could not, after all, have been chosen "because they suited the early church."[6] Clearly not. Either the Christians who wrote the

Gospels were all radical feminists, or they told the truth about how Jesus related to women.

The Middle Ages are often called the "Age of Faith." But the faith that dominated Europe after the fall of Rome was only one part Christian, and perhaps equal parts imperial cult, European paganism, and growing influence from the dominant religion of the time, Islam. The Bible may have been "the Book" to Europeans, but few could or were allowed to read it. Perhaps that is why women lost some power during this period. In some areas, the idea that land should only be passed on to sons caught on. Three quarters of the victims of witch hunts were women, except in a few countries such as Iceland. Indian women in Mexico seem to have done better before the Spanish appeared.[7]

But even in the Middle Ages, Muslim visitors were shocked by the freedom "Christian" women enjoyed. (Sometimes, as today, for destructive and non-Christian behavior.) And as literacy rose, and people began reading the Book, Jesus' example began to make a radical difference around the world.

Christian workers set up schools for women not only in Europe and the Puritan colonies (where literacy was close to universal), but in great literate civilizations such as China, India, and Japan, and among previously illiterate tribal peoples on every inhabited continent.

But maybe you missed all that. This is another part of history that is often sanitized for the general public.

## HOW HISTORY IS FALSIFIED

In September 2000, the *China Daily* carried a long article about how Chinese women had struggled against oppression during the millennia that had just ended. During the Song Dynasty (960–1279), a vogue for tying up the feet of young girls in cloth (foot-binding) caught on. As practiced in later centuries, four of a girl's toes would be broken, deforming her feet and hobbling her for life. The article made it sound as if inspiration for banning this cruel practice blew in out of the ether. "Chinese society didn't hear cries denouncing this discrimination against women until the turn of the [nineteenth] century," it claimed. The first school for women, the article added, opened in 1898.

Both claims are untrue. In fact, Christian missionaries began the struggle against foot-binding and for female education well before those dates. The first school for Chinese women opened in 1825 in Singapore—a full 73 years before the date reported by the official press. A second opened in 1844 in Ningpo (toward the coast from Shanghai), and then 17 more by the end of the century in ports open to foreigners. Shanghai historian Gu Weiming argues that these schools had a profound effect on Chinese society. Aside from providing education—the first step in liberating anyone—many of these schools refused to accept girls with bound feet.

Gu said missionaries were also instrumental in the movement to end foot-binding. "They believed that God created man as a whole, soul and body. To use unnatural means to injure and damage the body not only was inhumane, but contradicted Christian teaching."[8] The first society to end foot-binding was founded in 1874 in the city of Amoy (present-day Xiamen).

Would Gnostics have bothered? If flesh is a "prison," what harm if there is a little less of it below the ankle?

The great Chinese scholar Hu Shih understood better than the *China Daily* what brought change to China. Quoting a proverb, "Let women serve as oxen and horses," he said that women were treated with "meanness" in traditional China. For a thousand years, philosophers talked about benevolence but ignored "the cruel and inhumane treatment of their mothers and sisters." Then missionaries arrived. "They taught us many things, the greatest of which was to look at women as people."[9]

The gospel has served the same function around the world. But as in China, the facts are often suppressed. Often we are told outright lies, such as the *China Daily* claim that no one spoke up for or opened schools for girls in China until 1898. My female students in Japan didn't know that missionaries started the first schools for women there, too, or that they freed girls from forced prostitution. The only link in their minds between religion and women seemed to be the Taliban!

Americans, too, are told lies all day long on this subject, of which Dan Brown's and Tucker Malarkey's lies and the half-truths of Pagels, King, and Meyer are only the tip of the iceberg.

In India, women were often "deified in the abstract and demeaned in real life."[10] Indian Hindus agreed with Japanese Buddhists and Coptic Gnostics that a woman could only find salvation as a man. High-caste girls were often married before puberty to men in their forties and fifties. When her husband died, a girl was expected to throw herself on his funeral pyre and burn, too (a custom called *sati*). Female infanticide, the custom of demanding a heavy dowry from brides (which still makes Indians leery of raising girls), child marriage, and *sati* reflected a settled conviction that women were spiritually inferior.

Missionaries attacked each of these problems. An English shoemaker, William Carey, led the charge. One day, walking on the bank of a river with friends, he witnessed a woman being burnt to death with her dead husband. He begged the funeral company to let her go, warning them of God's judgment. The crowd shouted joyfully to Shiva and burned the woman to death. The couple's children were thus left not only fatherless, but orphans. Carey vowed to "hit this accursed thing hard, if God should spare him."[11]

In 1802, Carey was commissioned by the English government to investigate *sati*. He agitated for an end to the practice, and in 1829, it was banned (with the help of William Wilberforce and the "Clapham Sect" of evangelicals in England, who also ended the British slave trade).

These are just a few examples of a worldwide movement that,

I believe, goes far to explaining the United Nations figures. I suspect the status of women is lowest in many Muslim countries today not because Islam is intrinsically harsher toward women than Hinduism. Mohammed could be cruel—taking to bed the widow of a man his troops had just killed earlier that same day, for example—but Islam at least admitted that women were spiritual and fully human. The Muslim world has fallen behind, I think, because it rejected the cultural influence of Christianity more vigorously than other civilizations.

## JESUS IS GOOD FOR WOMEN

My conclusion is that faith in Jesus is good for sex, the female sex in particular. (Nor have I even had to resort to asking, "If Christianity is so bad for sex, why are there so many Christians?" Though there is some sense to that question, too.) Both Gnostics and orthodox Christians of long ago had bad attitudes to shake, including the common "spiritual" contempt for women and sexuality. But the best "feminist" scenes in the Gnostic writings involve Mary Magdalene because Jesus was in fact kind and respectful to her. Orthodox Christians such as Jerome were also challenged by his example.

In the West, women regularly serve in Congress, and 60 percent of undergraduates are female. What hurts us most is sexual exploitation. Nature binds women closely to children, and both suffer in particular when families break up. Here, Jesus rebukes us, too. Not only does he save a woman about to be stoned (which still makes him a busybody in northern Nigeria), he then tells her something that draws down the wrath of modern Americans: "Go and sin no more."

A pastor friend took a group of young people on a hiking trip. When he learned that one couple was sleeping together, he canceled the trip and told the parents of the two youths what happened. They reacted in opposite but equally cruel ways. The girl's father punched her in the face, gave her a black eye, and said, "You'll never darken the door of a church again!" The boy's mother threatened to sue the pastor for interfering with his social life. "If he wants to sleep with every girl in the youth group," she ranted, "that's none of your business!"

Jesus rebukes both parents. To the angry father he says, "Let he who has no sin throw the first punch." To the angry mother he says, "Teach your son to go and sin no more."

Jesus said, "Behold, I stand at the door and knock" (Revelation 3:20). Sometimes he has to stand there a long time. Sometimes our ears clang with uncomfortable truth for years before we undo the latch. A society may pray to Jesus for centuries before it begins to listen to him on such personal levels—and what one generation learns, the next may forget.

# 10

# GNOSTICISM WOULD NOT
# SET THE WORLD FREE

THE FIRST *MATRIX* MOVIE brilliantly updated the Gnostic myth for a technological age. In the story, Thomas Anderson (also called Neo) learns that the life he knows is unreal. The truth is spelled out in conversation with a man named Morpheus (the god of dreams in Greek mythology). Morpheus explains that the Matrix surrounds all of us. We feel it at work, in church, and when forking our funds over to the IRS. It keeps us from realizing the truth about our situation: that we are slaves. We are slaves confined not by bars or chains, but by the lies our minds accept as reality.

*Thomas* is, of course, the name of the most famous Gnostic text. In another Nag Hammadi writing, *Thomas the Contender,* Jesus instructs the disciple to flee involvement with the material realm. Jesus calls Thomas "my twin" and tells him "examine yourself and learn who you are" (NHL: 201). *Thomas* means "twin" in Aramaic, which is why, Pagels suggests, the Gospel was attributed to Thomas: By meeting Christ, "one may come to recognize oneself and Jesus as, so to speak, identical twins."[1] The person who knows himself comes to know "the depth of all things."

Morpheus also brings a message about "knowing who you are"

and thus learning "the depth of all things." He offers Thomas two pills—one red, one green. The green one will make him forget their conversation. The red one will open him up to the truth. Swallowing the pill, Neo finds himself gliding down his own throat into another and horrific world.

*Andros* is Greek for "man," so Neo's last name, Anderson, can be translated "son of man," a title both the apostles and the Gnostics applied to Jesus. To underline the point, at the beginning of the film. Neo helps a friend with computer software, who thanks him and compares him to Jesus Christ. To make identity between Neo and Christ clearer still, at the end of the movie, he comes back to life.

Neo is, as Morpheus promises, set free. The red pill frees him from the Matrix, the virtual reality program that images our world and controls us. Soon he is walking on walls (if not water), dodging bullets, and soaring into the sky like a rocket. He can't do this in the "real world"—a dreary dystopia in which machines with tentacles hunt the last humans in their holes—but in the fake digital world we inhabit, imaged and ruled by creators of the Matrix.

The Gnostic Jesus also offered freedom to escape this world. Jesus tells James, "I tell you this, that you may know yourself" (NHL: 35). Knowing oneself, and "the truth"—that life is a dream, a delusion created by archons who have caught us in "nets of flesh"—one ascends through many adventures to a higher plain of reality, to the peace and light of the "pleroma."

As one ascends, usually after death (or in out-of-body experiences), one rises to seven "heavens," in which archons punish the wicked. In eighth and higher levels, one escapes their baleful influence.

Gnostics saw orthodox Christianity as an enemy of freedom. Morpheus's lip, too, curls as he mentions church. He adds that Thomas pays taxes, underlining his reference to power structures that bind us. Some Gnostics saw themselves as part of the church and depicted the orthodox as just slow to awaken. But others saw the orthodox as more deeply in bondage to the Hebrew God, the "chief archon."

The cynical language of the Gnostics about authorities and powers holding the world in bondage merges easily with postmodern sensibility.[2] As Steve Emmel put it, "The authors of these texts were partly very smart people who found the simple faith a bit laughable."[3]

In *The Gospel of Thomas: The Hidden Sayings of Jesus,* eminent scholar Harold Bloom makes the case for the Gnostic Christ in terms he thinks will resonate with Americans. He praises *Thomas* for sparing Jesus (and us) the crucifixion, "and making the resurrection unnecessary." In *Thomas,* Jesus is "unsponsored and free." (One thinks of that preeminent American hero, Huck Finn, drifting down the Mississippi River.) No one was or could have been burnt at the stake "or even scorned" in the name of this Jesus.[4]

The dark view behind this last comment of the Christian effect on freedom has been common since the Enlightenment, when Voltaire described the church as *"L'Infame."* An anarchist friend told me he disliked religion for two related reasons. First, it is a "political tool" by which an "elite few" control many, and "therefore an enemy of freedom." Also, religion promotes "sloppy, non-critical thinking" which "fosters ignorance and intolerance, which are also ultimately enemies of freedom."

In recent years, a number of writers have worried that conservative Christianity either is or has always been a threat to freedom. Evangelicals, the "American Taliban" some have called them, aim to tear down the wall of separation between church and state and institute theocracy.

Some suggest that Gnosticism may be more liberating. In *Thomas,* Bloom argued, what makes people free is *gnosis,* or hidden knowledge, available to "every Christian, Jew, humanist, skeptic."[5] Truth is not doled out by a hierarchy of priests, bishops, and popes who offer salvation only to those who toe the line. The influential scholar Burton Mack described Jesus as a "cynic sage," a traveling Greek philosopher.[6] Bloom suggests that the real Jesus was neither a Christian nor the founder of Christianity, but "unsponsored and free." Perhaps *Thomas* reveals the true Jesus, a "wisdom teacher, gnomic and wandering," rather than "a proclaimer of finalities."[7]

Neo-Gnostics generally agree, then, on three facts. First, freedom is wonderful. Second, Christianity threatens it. And third, Gnosticism might open the bars of our prison.

I agree with the first point, though I think the Huck Finn model is too simple. The other two "facts," I will argue, are deeply mistaken.

I do not think an alternative Gnostic world would be a freer place. In fact, I find hints in Nag Hammadi literature that the search for *gnosis* would have liberated the West no more than the parallel search for enlightenment-liberated India—very little.

By contrast, I will argue, nothing has freed this world (I can't speak for the next one) more than the gospel of Jesus. The Bible is mankind's true Manifesto of Liberation. Almost every movement that actually liberated was set in motion by the Christian faith.

But first, let's look more closely at what freedom means.

## WHAT IS FREEDOM?

When I asked my anarchist friend what he meant by freedom, and why he liked it, he seemed surprised. We all love freedom, but often don't stop to define it. What is wrong, he finally replied, is compelling other adults to do what they don't want to do.

This definition is not very practical. For example, if you think compulsion is always wrong, what do you do at a stop sign? Do you stop, and give in to the Powers That Be? Perhaps in a world of pure spirit, cars go through one another, like ghosts at Hogwarts School for Wizards. But in our world, running stop signs leads not to freedom, but to confinement in plaster or a small pine box.

I write this a few days after a terrific windstorm downed power lines throughout the Pacific Northwest. I did feel a slight sense of liberation the first time I drove through a major intersection at my discretion. But gridlock—that is, loss of freedom—has been the usual result of this "gain" in freedom. It was with relief—not that of a slave returning to its master, but of an exile returning to the delicate web of delegated authority we call civilization—that we saw the first traffic light where power had been restored. The laws of physics in a material universe make rules necessary, and in specialized society liberty is gained for all when a few (who are, in turn, under democratic rule) make, apply, and enforce them.

Authority, said the apostle Paul, is instituted by God (Romans 13:1). While kingdoms may be "small robberies," as Augustine of Hippo put it, in any group the size of a family or larger, power must be delegated, or life grounds to a halt. Lines of authority run in different directions, though. Power eventually accrues to anyone who works and develops competence. A high school boy mopping a floor at McDonalds sets up a "wet floor" sign to defend his fiefdom from defiling shoes. If Ray Kroc, the founder of McDonalds, were still alive to visit, he would walk around the wet area—or risk bruising his wealthy behind.

Freedom cannot, then, be absolute. Most often it depends on delegated authority.

One day my anarchist friend visited a rural bar with an African-American girlfriend. On the door he found a sign letting black people know, in crude language, that they were not welcome.

Enraged, my friend sued. The bar owner lost, closed shop, and moved out of state. My friend, who has a strong sense of social justice, was proud of having run a racist out of business. He saw intuitively that freedom must be balanced by other values, and that sometimes in a world of sinners (though he disliked that word, too), it is right to compel others.

The Bible talks a lot about freedom. As we will see, the greatest movements for freedom have been inspired by the gospel. But orthodoxy depicts liberty as one in a rich ecosystem of values, not a lone-wolf virtue scavenging its solitary way across a denuded spiritual landscape.

Moral rules are internal road signs. As I argued in the last chapter, the "freedom" to copulate with anyone at any time is restricted for good reason: Indulgence in bed leads to more death and mayhem than indulgence on the highway. In a complex and dangerous material world, we find freedom through obedience: obeying stop signs, cops (usually), professors (in their area of authority), grocery clerks (lining up where they tell us to), wives, husbands, farmers at you-pick farms, and so on. Limits can be fun, which is why children make tunnels, tents, and forts. G.K. Chesterton pointed out that the best part of *Robinson Crusoe* was the list of things the hero scavenged from his ship. Life without limits is a bore.

Technological democracy restrains us at every turn and gives us freedom to do things jungle tribesman can't even dream about, such as visit the next village safely. It is a shallow heresy to suppose that social control, rule, hierarchy, and even obedience (how the word makes us shudder!) are always impediments to freedom. Religion might involve all these things and still liberate. Or it might erase all boundaries and enslave us.

## DOES GNOSTICISM LIBERATE?

Gnostic texts talk a lot about freedom. And it is probably true, as Bloom points out, that no inquisitors quoted *Thomas*. They didn't read him. Manichean Gnostics gained power only in Mongolia and some other parts of Central Asia.

But as I read Nag Hammadi literature, I find at least five signs that Gnosticism would not have made us more free. Gnosticism undercuts freedom both socially and technologically.

First, the Gnostics despised this world. Indian philosopher Vishal Mangalwadi asked why Hindu gurus did not challenge infanticide and *sati*. The problem, he concluded, was that life was not sacred. If life is "a bondage" or illusion,[8] why prolong it? Gnostic texts speak of salvation *from* this world, not about improving the things *in* it. It is hard to see how they would have done the latter.

Second, Gnosticism discouraged freedom by ignoring morality. Apart from three Christian or Jewish texts, less than one percent of Nag Hammadi material even weakly suggests we should do good. Not one piece of thoughtful moral advice can be found in any Gnostic text.

What, you may ask, do ethical rules have to do with freedom? Doesn't freedom mean not being told what to do? Didn't Huck Finn yearn to escape the Widow Douglas and her rules?

The truth is, morality nourishes freedom, even on the Mississippi River. Because the escaped slave Jim was honest, apart from "borrowing" melons from farmers, Huck could leave his raft on the riverbank and go into town without it being stolen.

Also, morality is discipline, and discipline brings freedom. Feed a child, put fencing between her and the highway, make her sit at a desk and do math when she wants to watch cartoons, and she internalizes constraint and diligence. Balance that discipline with play, and she grows up and learns to plot a rocket's trajectory to the moon—or a weekend on the Oregon coast. A slaver puts men in chains because he doesn't want them to be free. But a parent restricts her children so they can leap tall buildings in a single bound. By failing to discipline our conscience, Gnosticism may weaken our spirits.

Third, among ancient Greek, Roman, Indian, and Chinese intellectuals, *work* was a four-letter word. *Hypostasis of the Archons* suggests that some Gnostics felt the same way: "Moreover they [the archons] threw mankind into great distraction and into a life of toil, so that [they] might be occupied by worldly affairs, and might not have the opportunity of being devoted to the holy spirit" (NHL: 165). Physical labor, it seems, distracts us from spiritual pursuits. The Manichean elect were not allowed to grow crops, which were grown for them by lay "auditors" so they would not have to defile the divine light thought to be distributed in foods.[9]

Rodney Stark points out that traditional societies loved to consume, but were contemptuous of the labor that created consumable goods: "Notions such as the dignity of labor or the idea that work is a virtuous activity were incomprehensible in ancient Rome or in any other precapitalist society."[10] Grunt work should be left to lower castes or slaves when possible. The noble were thus freed to seek "spiritual" wisdom.

One of the turning points in history came when the apostle Paul said we should work with our hands. "If anyone is not willing to work, then he is not to eat" (2 Thessalonians 3:10). Paul did not merely give this advice, he followed it, making tents in his spare time. (When he wasn't fleeing mobs and wild beasts, preaching, founding churches, or writing the Bible!) This concept would have a profound effect. Because of the revolutionary idea that labor was sacred, Western monks worked with their hands. Among the hands they worked with were those on clocks: To regulate prayer and make work productive, monasteries invented elaborate timepieces and other machines.

Even though many or most monks and nuns were from the nobility or wealthy families, they honored work both theologically and by doing it. Saint Benedict, the founder of Benedictine monasteries, wrote that "the brothers" needed "specified periods" for work as well as study. "Idleness is the enemy of the soul.... When they live by the labor of their hands, as our fathers and the apostles did, then they are really monks."[11] Organized (i.e., "coerced"), stable, and increasingly wealthy monasteries created technology. The Christian view of work led both to the first great civilization not built on the back of slaves (medieval Europe), and eventually, to labor-saving devices that liberate us all.

The Gnostics didn't seem to notice that the apostles were fishermen or that their Lord was a carpenter. If they had, perhaps we would find a "Joseph Gospel" in which Jesus' spirit left his carnal image-body to split stones and hoist wood in his father's workshop while he chuckled in the shadows with a cool glass of spirit-lemonade in hand.

Fourth, Gnosticism would not have truly liberated people because it ignored underdogs. People were not created equal. Males were superior to females. *Zostrianos* said some existed "with souls" and others without them (NHL: 420). *On the Origin of the World* mentioned four races: three belonging to the king of the eighth heaven, and the fourth "kingless and perfect." The latter were immortal, and therefore "kings within the mortal domain" (NHL: 188). So some, it seems, were destined by nature to reign. Here we see an arrow pointing in the same direction that Aristotle followed when he said that some are slaves by nature, and that led Indian religion into the caste system.

Early Indian religion was fairly egalitarian. But a little before the time of Christ, the theory evolved that different castes had emerged from the body of God: Brahmin (priests) from his mouth, Rajanya (rulers) from his arms, Vaisya (warriors) from his thighs, and Sudra (servants) from his feet. Each caste was fixed into a corresponding slot in society. A quarter of the people were "outcaste," not from God at all. For 2000 years, they cleaned toilets, buried the dead, and lived in slums. Their very shadow was thought to defile a Brahmin. The Gnostics, it seems, had begun to divide mankind into similar unequal teams.

A final danger sign in Nag Hammadi is how the boundary between guru and god is sometimes erased. Jesus said "Render to Caesar the things that are Caesar's; and to God the things that are God's" (Matthew 22:21). *Thomas* added the words, "And give me what is mine" (NHL: 137). The history of esoteric religion teaches that when gurus begin to talk like that, hang on to your daughters, wallets, and liberty.

Western Gnosticism produced no dictators—nor did it have the chance. In Asia, where they were more successful, pantheistic and mystical doctrines seldom put any obstacle in the path of tyrants. *Gnosis* encourages "good men to do nothing" in an illusory world, put faith in the elect, and dream one's way to the promised land. It is a short step from belief in spiritual, psychic, or material tribes to believing that slaves were made to serve us, like Gammas, the lowest genetically engineered caste in Aldous Huxley's novel *Brave New World.* Otherworldliness, aversion to labor, disinterest in kindness, and contempt for common humanity is not a recipe for freedom.

Ironically, not even *The Matrix* paints much of a vision of freedom. Zion turns out to be an oligarchy with orgies and no sky, trees, flowers, or bees. The only food is tasteless protein gruel. Everyone wears biker black and lives in a hole under the earth. A more claustrophobic paradise would be hard to find. Nor do the inhabitants of Zion escape authority; one crew rebels against Morpheus's heavy hand.

Gnostic texts promise spiritual freedom and tell us heaven is a realm of perfect happiness. Others say one merges with the "true Father," or "the One." Maybe so! Not having ascended to the eighth heaven and seen for myself, I can't say it's not there—and I'm not sure anyone who has had such an experience, I will argue later, can say for sure that it is. But the tree seems rather barren to bear such sweet fruit.

# 11

# JESUS BRINGS
# TRUE FREEDOM

HISTORY IS LIKE the cartoon closet in which you can find anything you want. Whisper "history of Christianity" to some people in their sleep, and they'll mumble back, "Inquisition." Piety can be the ugliest form of blasphemy, and Fyodor Dostoyevsky's *Grand Inquisitor* stands firmly fixed in the Western imagination, along with Crusaders sacking Jerusalem and the house arrest of Galileo as symbols of Christian oppression. But proportion is everything in history. In fact, one Russian atheist, Joseph Stalin, killed as many innocent people on an average winter day of his 25-year career as all Spanish inquisitors in 300 years. That is a fact. A few flakes of snow on the summit of Kilauea does not make Hawaii a glacier. Nor will the breath of a passing sled dog melt the Greenland icecap.[1]

In the last chapter, I pointed to Gnostic qualities that might inhibit freedom: otherworldliness, lack of social passion, aristocratic laziness, the idea that some people are born better than others, and deference to gurus. The Bible warns us against these errors. Jesus told us to pray that God's will be done "*on earth* as it is in heaven" (Matthew 6:10). The prophets burn with passion for the poor and weak. Paul said we should work with our hands, and

Jesus and Paul did. The Bible anticipated modern genetics and denied a thousand forms of racism by asserting that all humanity is closely and recently linked through our primal ancestors.

Unlike Gnosticism, Christianity also has a long record in the real world to defend. Many people think that record is indefensible. Often even believers waive the question and say, "Sure, the Inquisition, the Crusades, Rhone River pograms, and your experiences with born-again bigots have been bad. Turn your eyes upon Jesus, and ignore his followers."

Many non-Christians are rightly impatient with such an answer. If God exists, and if he made this world and sent his Son to redeem it, surely the life of the Son of God should make some positive difference! Surely the gospel of Jesus ought to have done our planet some good! Jesus compared the kingdom of God to a shade tree that grows from a small seed. He also said we judge a tree by its fruit. Perhaps he was thinking of the trees in Ezekiel that grow beside a river flowing from the temple and bear fruit every season and bud leaves that heal. "Seed" also reminds us of God's promise to Abraham in Genesis, that through his seed all the families of earth would be blessed. If the tree of Christian history yields nothing but curled leaves and bitter fruit, what use is it? And why should we believe the kingdom of God has come?

My reply must be limited. I won't try to prove that no one has ever lynched an innocent person on the "tree of life." Human beings are geniuses when it comes to justifying evil. The higher the ideal, the more likely that it will be abused. Jesus himself warned that fools would twist the Word of God to persecute the innocent.

My argument will be more positive, and almost as ambitious. First, I'll show that freedom is central to biblical thought. Then I'll make the case that where liberty has taken root, its roots have most often drawn deeply from the river of Christian tradition.

## WHAT THE BIBLE SAYS ABOUT FREEDOM

In *The Tripartite Tractate*, the chief archon gives himself a slew of honorific titles. He creates "eternal punishments" for those who disobey. He appoints servants to do his will: The strong and arrogant are put in charge, those who lust for power are in mid-level positions, and those full of envy are put in entry-level "servile order" positions to command people who are controlled by lustful passion (NHL: 87). In *Apocryphon of John,* Yaltabaoth creates a whole hierarchy of spirits to subcontract construction of human organs.

What the imperial model of divine order misses is the freedom built into creation. How different is the picture scientists are coming to—a gradual creation and an exquisitely balanced cosmos in which "just right" laws of physics make life possible, yet in which not even the careers of subatomic particles are set in stone.

Genesis tells us the Creator took freedom seriously from the beginning:

> Then the LORD God took the man and put him into the garden of Eden to cultivate it and keep it....From any tree of the garden you may eat freely, but from the tree of the knowledge of good and evil you shall not eat, for the day that you eat from it you will surely die (Genesis 2:15-17).

Unlike the Gnostic or neo-Gnostic caricatures, the biblical account of creation bubbles over with intimations of freedom. God put Adam in Paradise. He had legs with which he could walk and hands with which he could grasp. (He was not the wimpy invertebrate of Gnostic myth.) Opposable thumbs gave him an advantage over other mammals. He could skin oranges, peel bananas, crack walnuts, lather up soap from one tropical tree and mosquito repellent from another, and tear wood or bamboo apart to make canoes, chopsticks, and fences. (Rousseau, who thought that first fence a mistake, probably never gardened.)

God gave Adam work to do: a "garden" that dwarfed an

Alaskan national park, with thousands of species. Adam was told to name these animals. (A job that humanity is still several million species shy of completing.) In the weighty shorthand of the opening chapters of Genesis, I believe this implies God wanted mankind to research creation, classify, and connect. Adam was commissioned as the first naturalist.

Living in material bodies in a universe with sharp edges has been compared to a fiddler playing music on a rooftop, trying to play a simple, pleasant tune without falling off and breaking his neck. Still, there was only one "stop sign" in Eden. God told Adam, of a particular tree, "The day that you eat from it you will surely die."

In *On the Origin of the World,* the forbidden tree is called the "tree of *gnosis.*" God wanted Adam to keep his hands off so he would remain ignorant. Yaltabaoth was afraid, like the machines that control the Matrix, that if clever man figured out the lie of the land, he might become a threat (NHL: 179-185). This is a popular human conceit. The ancient Greeks told the story of Promethius, a man at war with the gods. Karl Marx often quoted from that myth, including in his doctoral dissertation, and used it to chase God (or at least public worship of him) from one-third of the globe.[2] Through the systematic *gnosis* called science, some capitalists also cherish promethian ambitions.

We are free not only because (unlike limpets) we have limbs, eyes, and room to explore, but also because God told man what to do. The longest chapter in the Bible, Psalm 119, is an acrostic poem praising the wisdom and value of God's law: "I shall run the way of Your commandments. For You will enlarge my heart" (verse 32). Another translator renders this last phrase, "You have set my heart free." Breadth of space is one kind of freedom, and with a planet to themselves, the first man and woman had that. But God's law gives another kind of freedom. The book of James says "pure and undefiled religion" means "visit[ing] orphans and widows in their distress" (1:27). By setting bounds for freedom, and giving the free person useful things to do, whether tending a garden or helping the needy, God made man "king of infinite space," bounded though we were by matter.

Gnostics accuse Yaltabaoth of punishing Adam and Eve out of jealousy. He became angry because humans outsmarted him.

Why did God forbid the first couple the tree not of *gnosis* in general but of "the knowledge of good and evil"? One answer might be that parents hope their children won't learn everything the hard way! In his haunting retelling of the story of Eden, *Perelandra*, C.S. Lewis suggested that the issue at stake was not knowledge—which God was prepared to give, when the time was ripe—but obedience.[3] Obedience is faith in action, and faith—I will argue in the next chapter—is the purest act of reason. For example, we tell our children to come home at a godly hour because they are vulnerable and we love them. If your fairy godmother gives you a gown, a coach, horses, and ticket to the ball, hasn't she earned the right to set a curfew? Might not the Creator also limit in order to liberate?

Given Paradise, it seems ungrateful to pine over one tree. And even that *verboten* can be understood as part of God's gift of freedom. To be free, one must have choices. And choices must have consequences. This is a freedom materialists often deny, saying our paths are set by fate, electrons, society, economics, sex, or genes.

Paradise was lost, but God did not give up on liberty. In Deuteronomy, after teaching the ethics that give freedom—do not steal, lie, mislead a blind man on the road, worship idols, or take bribes—God again offers Israel a choice: "I have set before you life and death, the blessing and the curse. So choose life" (Deuteronomy 30:19).

Through the prophet Samuel, God warns his people not to adopt the dominant political pattern of the Middle East. If they choose a king, he says, taxes will increase, and children will be taken for corvee labor. Throughout the Old Testament, God is described as One who executes justice for the oppressed, gives food to the hungry, and sets prisoners free. Divine statutes set part of each crop aside for the poor. In the year of Jubilee, land was to be returned to its original owners. Prophets rebuked kings as they almost never did in Egypt or India, and rarely in China. In *Freedom, a History,* historian Donald Treadgold argued that the concept of freedom "comes from the Jewish religion." In addition, Hebrew society, "was unique in the ancient Near East in managing finally to avoid the techniques, devices, and institutions of despotism."[4]

Gnostics and postmodernists are right to be suspicious of power. The aphorism "Power tends to corrupt, and absolute power corrupts absolutely" was coined by Christian historian Lord Acton, and echoes God's warning to the children of Israel.

There was also a political element to the freedom Jesus offered. "Render to Caesar the things that are Caesar's; and to God the things that are God's," he said (Matthew 22:21). So the Christian stops at the stop sign, which is not erected just to keep him in bondage. He pays taxes, obeys parents, comes to work on time, and listens to his wife and even children in their spheres of responsibility. ("No forks tonight, Dad; we're having noodles.") But he also recognizes higher authority and obeys it when conflict arises.

The ancients spoke of fate and the stars, and behaviorists and Marxists agree our consciousness is determined.

For Christians, freedom is not a slogan we adopt to appeal to a democratic age, in the way that Lenin sprinkled insincere talk about "democracy" into his propaganda. Liberty is knit in many strands into the fiber of our faith. Nor is this just abstract theology. Almost every great historical movement for liberty has originated in Christian faith, as I will demonstrate shortly.

Of course this is to say nothing about what to do when the Christian love for freedom conflicts with other important values, such as justice—as with the racist bar owner or the government mandate to protect the innocent, which most Christians believe the debate over abortion involves. Nor would it be wise to say more now. Clearly, freedom is not the only issue, even for anarchists. The equally clear point at present is that freedom is terribly important to Christian theology.

## CHOOSING "THE BETTER PART"

Christianity enhanced freedom first of all by teaching people to read and write. Most civilized faiths emphasize education, if for no other reason, so people will read holy writ. But Christian teachers have been especially busy. It was they who invented the university. Christian scholars not only founded elite schools such as Oxford, Harvard, and Yale, but colleges and elementary schools that educate children of all classes on every continent. I mentioned the role missionaries played in teaching girls in China, India, and Japan. My wife, raised in a Buddhist family, went to Christian schools in Japan, as do millions of other non-Christian children. An educated person is often a fool, but he is a fool with more choices, and therefore more freedom, than an unread fool.

### *Slavery*

Jesus spoke once in the synagogue in his hometown of Nazareth. While there, he read from the glorious opening passage of Isaiah 61:

> The Spirit of the Lord God is upon me, because the Lord has anointed me to bring good news to the afflicted; He has sent me to bind up the brokenhearted, to proclaim liberty to captives and freedom to prisoners; to proclaim the favorable year of the Lord (verses 1-2).

Putting the scroll down, Jesus announced, "Today this passage has come true in your hearing."

Slavery was almost universal at the time of Christ. Jesus did not condemn slavery out-and-out, and it took the world some time to catch his drift. Great philosophers from Aristotle to Hume thought it a great idea to let inferior races do the work. Historian Paul Johnson called Christianity "the one great religion which had always declared the diminution, if not the final elimination, of slavery to be meritorious."[5]

Followers of Jesus ended slavery at least twice. In a key engagement in what could be called the first abolition movement in 1572, Admiral Don John defeated the Turkish fleet at Lepanto, freeing 15,000 oarsmen. G.K. Chesterton's poem "Lepanto" celebrates the day:

> Thronging of the thousands up that labour under sea
> White for bliss and blind for sun and stunned for liberty.
> *Vivat Hispania!*
> *Domino Gloria!*
> Don John of Austria
> Has set his people free!

Medieval Europe was the first great civilization not built on the backs of slaves. Indoctrinated in the precept that there was no favoritism with God, Christians slowly came to the conclusion that all men are brothers. Thomas Aquinas deduced that slavery was a sin. It was not a sin often committed in his day; slavery had long since become a rarity in most of Western Europe.

In 1402, the Spanish began to conquer the Canary Islands off the northwest coast of Africa and enslave its inhabitants. Pope Eugene IV issued a bull threatening to excommunicate the guilty parties, and giving them 15 days to restore liberty to the captives. That and later edicts were ignored, and within a century or so, Europe was back in the slave business with a vengeance. (At least one other pope would issue a bull justifying slavery, however.)

The great monotheistic civilizations mined Africa for labor, taking millions of slaves, starting wars, and leaving corpses strewn from the Sahara to the Atlantic. When Jesuits read a bull condemning slavery in Rio de Janeiro, rioters attacked their college. In 1700, Samuel Sewall, a Puritan judge, wrote a tract against slavery. By 1790, slavery was illegal in Massachusetts. About the same time a young English politician named William Wilberforce came to believe God had called him to end the slave trade. The elderly John Wesley wrote him, "Unless God has raised you up for this very thing, you will be worn out by the opposition of men and devils, but if God be for you who can be against you?"

The second abolition was also a Christian movement, preached in biblical language and supported almost entirely by zealous Christians both in America and England.[6] Almost 60 percent of agents for the American Anti-Slavery Society were pastors.

It was also under the political and moral pressure of the gospel that slavery was banned in Muslim, Chinese, and Hindu lands. Even today, Christians remain at the forefront—fortunately, no longer alone—of combating new forms of human trafficking.

### Setting Captives Free

The Salvation Army publicly shamed the peoples of England and Japan into ending forced prostitution. Today, members of the International Justice Mission engage in sting operations to liberate young women. I have visited Christian centers in Thailand, the Philippines, Japan, and Taiwan that have brought freedom to hundreds of prostitutes.

As we saw, missionaries liberated women in many ways—through education, allowing women the freedom to choose marriage partners or marry late, and by helping end sati, polygamy, infanticide, and foot-binding. One missionary, commissioned to help implement the Chinese government's new policy against foot-binding, grouched, "If God intended little girls to have horribly stubby little feet, he'd have made them like that in the first place!"[7] Aside from doing more than anyone to end slavery,

William Wilberforce made it his habit at mealtime to read the names of Indian widows who had been burnt to death and pray for them.

The caste system in India was one of the most oppressive control mechanisms the world has ever seen. Only about three percent of Indians belonged to the highest caste. One-fifth were outcastes, now about 200 million people.

The gospel hit Indian consciousness with a shock that reverberates to this day. William Carey, the founder of modern missions, was a one-man dynamo of reform. He studied India's plant life, advocated for lepers, founded Asia's first college, and found husbands for widows saved from immolation. First missionaries, then Indians, began to crusade against long-accepted injustices. The greatest nineteenth-century Indian reformer, Ram Mohan Roy, saw himself as calling Hindus back to one God. He published extracts of the gospels under the title, *The Principles of Jesus, the Guide to Peace and Happiness*—a title that accurately reflected the place those principles played in his own reform program. At the end of the study *Modern Religious Movements in India*, which tells the story of religious reform to the time of Gandhi, J.N. Farquhar concluded by describing Christianity as "a great searchlight" that revealed India to herself, showing her where she needed reform.[8]

Farquhar showed that early Indian reformers, whether or not they called themselves Christian, generally believed in one God. Christian influence led them to abandon polytheism, idol worship, and the worship of gurus. They were especially touched by the example of Jesus. "Feeble attempts" were sometimes made to trace these ideas to Hinduism, but informed people understood that reform had been introduced by missionaries. Some Hindu movements even jettisoned such core ideas as reincarnation and karma. Farquhar argued that these concepts were especially anti-Christian, for reasons that should interest the student of Gnosticism:

For it involves not only the theory that each individual passes through many lives and deaths, but also the doctrines that a man's place in society is an infallible index of the stage of soul-progress he has reached; that the suffering he undergoes is strictly equivalent to his past sins; that women are born women because of former sin, that to seek to ameliorate the social condition of an individual or a tribe is futile...that divine forgiveness is impossible; and that, since God stands apart from karma, He is necessarily actionless.[9]

How familiar this sounds! God does not act in this world. Women are inferior. Charity will harm your soul. Sex is evil, or (tantric Hindus would say) the path to salvation. Souls return to new bodies. Helping outcastes is spiritually harmful. Some people are just born better.

What bitter irony that some think Gnosticism, which preached many of the doctrines that enslaved India, should be our salvation! And that they scorn the gospel, which has done more than anything else to liberate humanity!

## POLITICAL FREEDOM

"Rebellion to tyrants is obedience to God," said Benjamin Franklin. The apostle Peter wrote on freedom in a way that might seem like nonsense to modern Americans. "Submit yourself for the Lord's sake to every human institution," he said. "Act as free men, and do not use your freedom as a covering for evil, but use it as bondslaves of God" (1 Peter 2:16). To us this sounds like George Orwell's slogan "Freedom is slavery," and the term "bondslaves" sets our teeth on edge. But why is it that rebellion against God, in the French, Russian, or Chinese revolutions, led to such appalling tyranny, while the American Revolution, with "no king but king Jesus" (as John Adams put it), led to freedom? Perhaps America's founders understood the nature of freedom pretty well.

The early church was free in part because believers were willing to die. Justin Martyr told the emperor Titus, "You can kill us, but you cannot hurt us." He also warned, "You shall not escape the coming judgment of God if you continue in your injustice." Justin did not challenge the emperor's right to rule. But Christians set up a network of "little platoons" that softened absolute imperial power.

Pluralism developed slowly from small seeds. Western thinkers often quoted two of Jesus' aphorisms—"Render to Caesar the things that are Caesar's; and to God the things that are God's," and "My kingdom is not of this world" as the institutions of European liberty slowly grew and spread.

The gospel also played a role in protecting civilization from later forms of tyranny. First, after *jihad* swallowed Persia, India, and two thirds of Christendom, had the church not given Europe unity (and a sword!), we would all probably speak Arabic. Perhaps it is politically incorrect to say so, but I think being under *sharia* law would be even worse than being stuck in traffic with the street-lights off. Women, at any rate, might not be on the street at all.

A defining moment in Japanese history came in 1891 when a Christian teacher named Uchimura Kanzou refused to bow as an imperial edict was read at a Tokyo high school where he taught. Japanese papers reported the incident as a mark of Christian disrespect for the Imperial House. That was one of the first cracks in the edifice of totalitarian rule. Japanese Christians, many of them converts from the Samurai class, also helped free Japan from tyranny by creating trade unions and other "civil society" networks.

Nazi and Communist regimes channeled the Enlightenment toward new forms of paganism and put 100 million people in slave labor camps. Alexander Solzhenitsyn found Christ in one of them. Later he wrote of millions of Christians "like candles" who lit up the darkness of the Gulag. Great Christian leaders such as Solzhenitsyn, Lech Walesa, and Pope John Paul with other

Christians in the ranks behind them, helped end communism. The American and British firepower that checked Communist expansion and ended Nazi and Shinto slave empires was strengthened by the love of liberty that the gospel helped bring to the West, as well as by "just war" teaching that allowed us to take up arms in national defense.

Christianity may also help China find its way to liberty. Leaders of the illegal "house church" movement have issued manifestos chastising the state for not practicing separation of church and state, and warning authorities of "violating God's will to their own detriment" in a tone similar to that of Justin Martyr in the second century.

## FREEDOM FROM SIN?

Apologists for Communism sometimes spoke about "freedom from" as opposed to "freedom of." "Western countries emphasize freedom *of* the press," they would say. "But we have achieved freedom *from* poverty, poor sanitation, and racial discrimination, which our people care more about." In cynical moments, I am tempted to read this as, "We may be slaves, but at least we're fat ones."

But often people are enslaved by conditions that must be removed before they can enjoy freedom. Unless your computer is freed of viruses, you can't surf the Internet. After one is free *from* debt, one can take a tour of UNESCO World Heritage sites in India, or surf in Mexico, if one pleases.

Jesus said, "You will know the truth, and the truth will make you free" (John 8:32). "We've never been slaves," the congregation replied. "Everyone who commits sin is the slave of sin," Jesus explained. "If the Son makes you free, you will be free indeed" (verses 34,36). So freedom is more than just the ability to move unconfined, a limit to government snooping and greed, or "rules of the road" to avoid collisions. Freedom also has an internal component.

Some of the best stories are of liberation *from* designer archons: heroin, tobacco, lust, hatred, pride. How can we love others when we are enslaved to bad habits or selfish attitudes? Like a carburetor, the heart burns best when the guck is flushed out.

Christians ended slavery even while recognizing that the most crippling slavery is spiritual. How many people have found freedom just by obeying Jesus and forgiving an enemy? How many are free *from* STDs and *to* walk, climb, and take their kids on trips to Yellowstone National Park because they chose to "go and sin no more" sexually? Biblical stop signs give freedom not *from* the road (which means getting stuck in the mud), but *of* the road, to travel freely the law that liberates.

Speaking of automobiles, that reminds me of another great liberating movement: modern science. Because of technology, we live longer, eat better, travel farther, and understand more about our world. What is the relationship between faith, reason, and technological progress?

# 12

# MENIGGESSTROETH DIDN'T MAKE YOUR MIND

ANOTHER GREAT MODERN MYTH tells of war between faith and reason, or religion and science.

Those who believe this myth debate details. Richard Dawkins, Oxford biologist and probably the most famous proponent of atheism in the world, often makes three assertions. First, faith means "blind trust, in the absence of evidence, even in the teeth of evidence."[1] Second, in fact religious faith has no evidence to support it. And third, that makes it repugnant, "the great cop-out, the great excuse to evade the need to think and evaluate evidence."[2] The late Stephen Jay Gould, renowned Harvard zoologist who often sparred with Dawkins, in this case agreed with the first two points, but disputed the third. True, religion doesn't have any evidence to back it up, and shouldn't pretend to, he "conceded" (as an agnostic himself). But religion may still be of value. Faith and science are "non-overlapping magisterial (or 'teaching authority')." They cover different realms of thought. So long as religion sticks to "moral meaning and value," it might do some good. Gould found religion fascinating—almost as much so as evolution, paleontology, or baseball.[3]

Ironically, the myth of separation of church and mind is always, in my experience, taken on faith "in the teeth of" contrary evidence. Michael Shermer, editor of *Skeptic* magazine and a friend of Gould's, conducted a poll of American adults. He found that the most common reason people believed in God was the perception of design in nature. Shermer concluded that these believers were misinformed about the nature of belief. Pure Christian faith had somehow become contaminated with scientific rationalism. Oddly, even Pope John Paul II, whom one would expect to be an informed Christian thinker, made the same mistake. The pope described faith and reason as "inseparable."[4]

This myth has also crept into neo-Gnostic ideology. In fact, Dawkins and Pagels both quote the same epigram from the second-century writer Tertullian, in slightly different forms: "It is by all means to be believed because it is absurd" (Dawkins), and "It must be believed, because it is absurd!" (Pagels).[5]

That both the leading atheist and neo-Gnostic converge on a single quote is remarkable for three reasons. First, it is striking that, with 2000 years of theology and thousands of pages from the church fathers, both writers (and others) converge on this one phrase. It reminds me of the metaphor in which the state of Texas is covered with coins a foot deep, and a blindfolded man selects the only gold coin in the pile not once, but several times in a row. The coincidence is suspicious. Second, it is especially remarkable that scholars from Oxford and Princeton use this quote to (seemingly) represent the Christian position, because it probably did not even accurately represent Tertullian's position! I think Pagels knew this; but here she is trying to explain why the orthodox came to believe in the bodily resurrection of Jesus, which she also found absurd. She leaves the implication that the early Christians were drawn to absurdity for its own sake stand out like a fat hanging curveball. But this implication is not true. Third, it is especially significant because the context here is an argument with a Gnostic, Marcion, who said Jesus never came in the flesh. Here's more of the passage:

> The Son of God was crucified; I am not ashamed
> because men [must be] ashamed of it. And the Son of
> God died; it is by all means to be believed, because it
> is absurd. And He was buried, and rose again; the fact
> is certain, because it is impossible. But how will all this
> be true in Him…if He really had not in Himself that
> which might be crucified, might die, might be buried,
> and might rise again? *I mean* this flesh suffused with
> blood, built up with bones, interwoven with nerves,
> entwined with veins….

Now it seems to me that here, if nowhere else, scientists
and historians ought to be on Tertullian's side. Jesus was not a
phantom. He had a flesh-and-blood body. What did Tertullian
mean by saying it should be believed because it is absurd? Certainly not that the evidence that Jesus really died on the cross was
poor. Tertullian may be anticipating a form of the "argument from
embarrassment." Marcion thought Jesus could not have come in
the flesh because the material universe was shameful. Tertullian
replies, like Lao Zi, and how do you know the greatness of God
does not lie precisely in his humility? The apostles would not have
invented such a story because it shames our pride. But when we
are weak, he is strong.

But as the saying goes, a lie can get halfway around the world
while the truth is putting her boots on. In *The Da Vinci Code*,
while taking a short break from murdering people, the leader of
the Catholic fellowship Opus Dei stops to ponder, "Unbiased
science could not possibly be performed by a man who possessed
faith in God. Nor did faith have any need for physical confirmation of its beliefs."[6] The hero of *Resurrection* likewise tells her
Christian villain, who has matched Opus Dei drop for drop of
innocent blood: "They've been told to replace thought with faith.
A good Christian does not question. A good Christian accepts
what he is given. It does not matter if he understands it."[7]

The truth is, as usual, vastly different from the lies—more

subtle, but ultimately richer and more interesting. Faith and reason are not enemies at all. They are better described as lovers. Almost every religion demands reason, and every form of valid reasoning without exception lives only by faith. In Gnostic terms, Pistis (Faith) and Wisdom (Sophia) are consorts, and from their love, Truth is born. *Treatise on the Resurrection* says that someone who does not believe must lack the capacity to believe. "For it is the domain of faith, my son" (NHL: 55). But Gnostic faith, too, usually presupposes reason of a sort. The problem is that the kind of reasoning Gnostics engage in—direct mystical knowledge—is highly unreliable. Christianity both delights in reason and makes much better use of it. Aside from embracing historical truth, one use Christians put reason to is inventing the magisteria called *science*.

## THE MARRIAGE OF FAITH AND REASON

In the past, I've compared faith and reason to two chopsticks that are used in tandem to pick up a Chinese dumpling. Pope John Paul II compared them to the wings of a bird. The point in both cases is that faith and reason are "two modes of knowledge [that] lead to truth in all its fullness."[8] To know something, anything at all, we rely on one or more of four objects: the mind, the senses, other people, and God (each of which can be broken down further: faith in parents, brother, bosom friend, gossip friend, gossip friend after three drinks, and so on). The Christian idea of faith in God is almost exactly like the faith that leads scientists to trust their own minds, the unseen nerves that allow them to look, hear, feel, smell, and taste objects and the social interdependence that make terms such as *coauthor, review of the literature, technical support* and *peer review* important concepts in science. To scorn the trust of others is not considered especially rational in any field, but an act of professional suicide that will land you in a rabbit hutch in rural Montana.

But faith is never safe. Mind and senses deteriorate. People lie, exaggerate, mistag babies, and point to the wrong men in lineups. This is why faith requires reason, too. And sometimes, Faith goes on a blind date, and children named Ignorance and Error are born.

## LOOKING FOR TRUTH IN ALL
## THE WRONG ASHRAMS

Isn't it better to experience ultimate reality directly, rather than pore over dusty old documents or listen to Brylcreemed preachers? Mystics call this "biting the apple for yourself." Once you have experienced the truth, you will have no more doubts. The *Upanishads* say the sages were not satisfied with the lower knowledge given by ancient Indian religion, and went in search of "higher" *gnosis*—direct mystical experience. Some say it's time Christians do the same. A follower of the Indian guru Muktananda told me her friends have met Jesus in the spirit, and he is just as the Gnostics describe him.

But something bothers me. I have heard essentially the same line from Mormons, Moonies, Hindus, and yes, evangelical Christians. A "burning in the bosom" or the "unity state" or "biting the apple," and you *know*—and no one can dissuade you again. But God can't be all the things these different religions say he is! They badly contradict one another.

One weakness of the esoteric way of knowing is that until you have gotten your mouth around the apple (or pretend you have), you usually rely on someone else's experience. Trusting in the mystical claims of a guru is weaker than historical evidence of the kind found in the Bible for at least three reasons: First, most mystical experiences happen to a single person, while the biblical Gospels are (as we saw) corroborated by others. Second, mystical experience is subjective. Even if a shaman relates exactly what he saw, such as dreams, hallucinations, and mescaline trips (which Gnostic stories resemble), it happened in his head. How do we know the ascent described in *The Discourse of the Eighth and Ninth* or *The Apocalypse of Paul* occurred anywhere else—even if these stories were not invented, like so much of the so-called Jesus material getting attention these days?

Third, a lot of it obviously is made up. Mystics are seldom sticklers for history. The carelessness seems contagious. As we saw earlier, even leading neo-Gnostic historians seem strangely uninterested, at times, in "whether this really happened." Gnostics ask us to believe four things: 1) Their books really did come from Mary, Thomas, Judas, or Philip; 2) who really did meet Seth or Sophia; 3) who really were real; and 4) who really told the truth. All four links need to be strong, or the chain breaks. But every one of them is held together by wet napkins. The slightest tug, even from sympathetic scholars, and it all comes to pieces.

People do have mystical experiences of Jesus, but not always the real Jesus. I met a high school boy in Taiwan who told me the spirit inside him called itself Jesus, and sometimes the son of Matsu, the Chinese sea goddess. But while Matsu and Jesus both helped fishermen, otherwise the two were hard to connect. The young man didn't act like Jesus, either. He smoked heavily, tried to scare and manipulate his neighbors (and me), and talked calmly about stepping in front of cars. I came away skeptical about disembodied spirits that speak in the name of famous people.

After an abuse scandal at the Bay Area Ananda Society, a reporter asked why such scandals seem to occur at every commune in America. Part of the answer is that power tends to corrupt, and *guru* or *pastor* can be good career paths for upwardly mobile psychopaths. But if your philosophy allows, Hamlet's hypothesis is also worth considering: "The spirit that I have seen may be the devil…[which] abuses me to damn me." If there are lying spirits, as people around the world have always believed, that's another weakness in the chain of trust.

## CHRISTIAN FAITH AND REASON

Richard Dawkins defined faith as "blind trust, in the absence of evidence, even in the teeth of evidence."[9] Where did he get this idea? Not from Tertullian, whom he could not have read directly.

Great Christian thinkers have always held a vastly different view of faith and reason. The first Christian philosopher, Justin Martyr, said reason "directs those who are truly pious and philosophical to honor and love only what is true." Clement of Alexandria wrote of "faith through demonstration." Augustine said people who think Christians believe "without any proofs" (he could have had in mind many modern writers) are "much deceived." "Heaven forbid" we should believe without evidence, since it is rationality itself that allows us to believe. Tertullian called reason "a thing of God" since he used reason to create, destroy, and set all things in place.

Nor did Christian rationalism die with the Romans. Thomas Aquinas, the greatest medieval philosopher, argued that God could be proven through natural reason. John Calvin said reason distinguished man from the animals, and entitled a chapter in his chief work, "Rational Proofs to Establish the Belief of the Scripture." The great missionary Matteo Ricci promised his Chinese friends, "My explanations will be based solely on reason," begging them to point out any flaws in his argument. Johannes Kepler, in dabbling with the cosmos, echoed Augustine and Tertullian in saying that God was "supremely rational," and that was why man, made in his image, had reason, too. Therefore religion, which is about how God and man relate, "cannot be but rational." As his biographer, James Conner, put it, "For Kepler, God had planted truths in nature to act as a kind of wordless Scripture, a companion to the Bible."[10]

The same idea also appears (for Dawkins's convenience, if he would pay attention) among eminent Christian thinkers at his own university, Oxford. If he wanted to know what Christians thought about faith, why not ask colleagues? Alister McGrath, one of the world's leading theologians, rejects blind faith with contempt. McGrath pointed out that he had never even met a theologian who looked at faith that way.[11] Richard Swinburne, an imminent Oxford philosopher whom Dawkins pokes fun at in his new book, *The God Delusion,* said the "irrationalist spirit" is the true modern heresy.[12] Going back a few years, C.S. Lewis was the most famous Christian writer of the twentieth century and taught a few hundred yards from Dawkins's office. Lewis defined faith as "the power of continuing to believe what we once honestly thought to be true until cogent reasons for honestly changing our minds are brought before us."[13]

In fact, Dawkins defines Christian faith the way he does not only in the "absence of evidence," to use his own words, but "in the teeth of [a tremendous wealth of] evidence."

I pick on Dawkins and Pagels because as public and highly influential scholars at major universities they have a great responsibility to get things right. I am amazed at how broadly their ideas (and even how they express those ideas) carry on the wind of popular culture. For two millennia, the gospel has called men and women to faith supported by reason.

Of course, that doesn't mean our reasons for faith are sound. It may be that my arguments for the biblical Gospels carry deep flaws. Is the Christian reliance on history one such fatal flaw?

Experiencing God is important for Christians, too. But Christian faith is also about public knowledge. "This has not been done in a corner," the apostle Paul said of Jesus' death and resurrection (Acts 26:26). Many disciples were still alive, he pointed out, who had seen the risen Lord. The canonical Gospels, written while many of those who traveled with Jesus were alive, tell how his friends saw, talked, ate with, and touched Christ. Is it reasonable to base our faith on claims made by people we have not met and about events that happened long ago?

After painstakingly following many lines of evidence, N.T. Wright concluded that they converged on the fact that Jesus died and rose again. "The proposal that Jesus was bodily raised from the dead possesses unrivaled power to explain the historical data at the heart of early Christianity."[14]

Nor did any New Testament writer see the resurrection, as Pagels and others suppose, as just "spiritual," believing that Jesus rose as some sort of bodiless phantom. That was not, Wright concluded, what Paul or anyone else meant: "The idea of a non-bodily resurrection would have been as much an oxymoron to him as it would to both Jews and pagans of his day; whether you believed in the resurrection or not, the word meant bodies."[15]

Why does this matter? Christians believe in public, historical evidence about which we can debate. Like knights tugging on the sword Excalibur, historians have stepped up to the first-century evidence one by one, and tried to wrest the "historical Jesus" from his orthodox context to use as a weapon in some noble cause. But the heart of he who would draw this sword must be pure. The gospel pulls the sword smoothly from the stone, and places it back, to let skeptics test another theory.

Faith in other people is risky, but what can you do? Step into a car or an airplane, open a can of juice, turn on a stove, and you place your life in the hands of strangers. We do it every day. We also conduct national debates about countries for whose existence we rely entirely on the testimony of other people. Go to Iraq, and what you see and hear "directly" (by faith in a complex series of electromagnetic and chemical reactions in your head which few understand and fewer still have seen even through a microscope) is limited to the Green Zone of Baghdad, perhaps. In fact, no one knows "Iraq" or "America" directly. I only think that I was born in the United States because people tell me that.

Jesus said, "Blessed are they who did not see, and yet believed" (John 20:29). The author of Hebrews wrote, "Faith is the conviction of things not seen" (11:1). The point is not that we should believe without evidence. Rather, faith in those we have reason to trust expands our knowledge of the world. It is by the practice of reasonable faith that we live life to the full. Without it we are blind, deaf, dumb, and alone—and ultimately can't even be sure of our memory or power to think.

## WHERE SCIENCE CAME FROM

Sociologist Rodney Stark found that of the 52 greatest early scientists, 32 (61.5 percent) were pious believers. Eighteen were "conventionally" religious. Only two, Edmund Halley and Paracelsus, seem to have been skeptics.[16] The men who invented science took a lively interest in nature, which they called God's handiwork. In exploring the nature of gas, light, the cell (named after a monk's room), the elasticity of springs, or how the planets orbited the sun, they often saw themselves as "thinking God's thoughts after Him." Nature was comprehensible because God was the author of order and reason. Johannes Kepler, a faithful believer whose family suffered much from religious conflict, often expressed a delighted praise as he explored the secrets of the solar system, a study he undertook as worship:

> I strive to publish [my observations] in God's honor, who wishes to be recognized from the book of nature. But the more others continue in these endeavors, the more I shall rejoice; I am not envious of anybody. This I pledge to God, this is my decision. I had the intention of becoming a theologian. For a long time I was relentless: but now see how God is, by my endeavors, also glorified in astronomy.[17]

Science was born in a time and place during which the integrity of creation was taken for granted because people believed in a good Creator. But suppose Kepler saw nature as a trap. How would his research have gone if he believed the planets were hellish spheres where archons tortured the dead? Suppose he thought his brain was the work, as *Apocryphon of John* theorizes, of an archon named Meniggesstroeth, and that the right eye was produced by Asterechme, the left by Thaspomocha, the left ear by Bissoum, and the right ear by Yeronumos? The nervous system must have been parted out to dozens of district spirits. Would such quarrelsome imps get together to swap blueprints? Would they even want us to see the world as it is, anymore than the machine monsters in *The Matrix?* What would be the point of exploring such a phantom or deceptive universe? Without trust in the brain, senses, or natural world, it is hard to see how science could have gotten going.

Nowadays people of every and no beliefs do science, including many atheists and followers of mystical faiths. Once science was invented, it did not require Christian dogma to keep going. But scientists still work in the spirit, and under many of the assumptions, of Johannes Kepler: The universe obeys uniform laws everywhere, it is comprehensible, and what our mind and senses tell us about it can reasonably be trusted.

Physicist Brian Greene describes how he and his colleagues have learned more and more about the nature of matter in a book tellingly titled *The Elegant Universe.* He ends the book, like Kepler, in a fit of boyish exuberance:

> Whether any of our descendants will ever take in the view from the summit and gaze out on the vast and elegant universe with a perspective of infinite clarity, we cannot predict. But as each generation climbs a little higher, we realize Jacob Bronowski's pronouncement that "in each age there is a turning point, a new way of seeing and asserting the coherence of the world." And as our generation marvels at our new view of the universe—our new way of asserting the world's coherence—we are fulfilling our part, contributing our rung to the human ladder reaching for the stars.[18]

The coherence of the universe was a Christian dogma and a Gnostic heresy. It is a key requirement of every branch of science—something we take for granted, but our ancestors did not. Curiosity and delight in nature (neither worship nor contempt) need to be engrained in a young scientist or a scholar in any field. Gnostics sometimes make great poets and filmmakers, and interesting psychologists. But great science, history, or law was never done in the spirit of Gnosticism. Not just in Brian Greene's field of participle physics, but in every realm of thought, the world is a playing field that beckons the curious to come and explore, and makes an old man feel at death like a child called in too early to dinner.

If Gnosticism had won, the glorious, world-transforming enterprise of science could not have been born. It is a child of orthodox Christian faith.

# 13

# SPINNING JESUS

I ONCE COMMITTED an unintentional but highly successful act of identity fraud.

In the spring of 1986, after running out of money while studying in mainland China, I met a Taiwanese girl in Hong Kong. I told her I was planning to spend the summer in Taiwan, and she suggested I stay at China Evangelical Seminary. Students were off for the summer and a dorm room would be available. She told me to say hello to the seminary receptionist, a friend of hers.

I did as directed. Soon I found myself in the company of three lovely young ladies who treated me to delicious Chinese food almost every noontime and patiently engaged me in long conversations in my primitive Chinese. *What fine hosts the Taiwanese are!* I thought. And what a godsend! I didn't have enough money to eat out and was too clumsy to worry about overstaying my welcome. My Chinese seemed to make rapid advances. If their responses to attempts to flirt seemed a bit inscrutable, I put that down to the alien culture.

Later I learned the truth. The girl I'd met in Hong Kong also had an American boyfriend—her fiancé, in fact. The seminary girls assumed I was he, and saw it as their duty to entertain and educate their friend's betrothed.

Intentional identity theft can be an even more lucrative ruse. Thieves don't usually need to copy their target's voice, face, fingerprints, or retina pattern, as in a science fiction movie. Often Social Security or account numbers are good enough; the bank doesn't know you personally.

Identity theft is also common in religion. Often a century or two after a great teacher appears, competing gurus invent stories to put their precepts in his mouth. Such unpaid celebrity endorsements were common in ancient times, too. The philosopher Confucius made a huge impression on China 500 years before Christ. His kindly and sensible teaching was like a breath of fresh air in an age so cruel that rulers were known to use subjects for target practice. But 200 years later, intellectuals were ready to have some fun at the expense of a school that had earned a reputation for being straightlaced. In the Taoist book *Zhuang Zi*, Confucius sometimes became the straight man for humor. In other passages, he was made to talk like a Taoist sage: "Men do not mirror themselves in running water—they mirror themselves in still water. Only what is still can still the stillness of other things." Later, Taoists competed with a religion imported from India by claiming Buddha was only copying a travel-worn version of the teachings of their founding sage, Lao Zi. In modern China, entrepreneurs sell gold busts of Chairman Mao, inducing the arch-communist into peddling capital products.

Jesus is the most frequent target of this kind of identity theft. The reason is obvious. Spiritual thieves are not primarily after money (though often that, too), but souls. Jesus has inspired more people, changed more lives, been quoted by more people, and has better name recognition than, it turns out, the Beetles. The thief said he robbed banks because "that's where the money is." The gospel is where spiritual capital has been deposited, so this is where thieves break in and steal.

The history of Jesus frauds is long and rich. *The Gospel of Barnabas* presents Jesus as a kind of apprentice to Mohammed, yearning to be worthy to tie the great prophet's shoelaces. *The Aquarian Gospel* tells how Jesus ran off to India and Tibet. Hindus and Buddhists say he learned magic there; some New Agers have him educated in Egypt. *The Book of Mormon* tells how he went to South America to preach Yankee platitudes in King James English. Children of the Enlightenment eagerly remade Jesus in their own images: pragmatic teacher, proto-revolutionary, hippy in an age of Augustan yuppies, cynic sage. Gnostics made one of the first attempts to tame Jesus, to domesticate the lion of Judah and make him (as Dorothy Sayers put it) a "housecat for pale priests and pious old ladies" of all ages, genders and faiths.[1]

How do we know these alternative identities are false? First, because only a small amount of the evidence fits any of them. Occasionally the case for the fraudulent identity may be as strong as the case that I was my Chinese friend's fiancé. Both of us were American. Most scholars at least make their "historical Jesus" Jewish (though some of the "cynic sage" school do not). All borrow the name, which I did not. Some thieves attempt to copy Jesus' wisdom, others his concern for the marginalized, others his aphoristic genius or talent at parables or "kingdom stories." But most just borrow a few set phrases, such as "Blessed is," or an event or two in his life. One skeptic made Jesus a miracle-worker, or magician (he said it didn't matter which). Others gave him wild eyes and put a sign in his hands, "THE END OF THE WORLD IS NIGH!" Many borrowed a radical antidisestablishmentarianism and made Jesus a rebel against class and hierarchical oppression. Still others called him the original feminist.

Bits and pieces of truth do not make a theft honest (though some may be unaware that they are committing fraud, as I was). The resemblance is superficial—like copying someone else's phone number or Social Security number on a form. Few of these "copy Jesuses" would fool anyone who knows the real Jesus. The face is different. Even the cleverest "historical Jesus" scholar sacrifices too much of the Gospels' portrait to in-house dogmas—miracles don't happen, the disciples were into spin, Jesus could not have identified himself with God. At worst—as in the case of Gnostic Gospels—Jesus becomes a mere stick-figure Savior who cannot hold up for a second to the extraordinarily rich and multilayered figure we find in the true Gospels.

What about the orthodox Jesus? Is he a figure created by theological spin, too? Doesn't every Christian denomination also stress certain aspects of Jesus' character (and of God's), and neglect others? Sometimes, no doubt. One might convict Constantine of committing identity theft when he painted crosses on his army's shields and rode out to "conquer by this." And what of the captain who brought the first black slaves to America on a ship named the Good Ship Jesus? Identity theft is endemic in "Christian" history, and I cannot claim to be innocent.

Berate we who bear the name of Christ dishonorably if you like. If you run out of rhetorical stones, pick up the Bible. The prophets rebuked the Jews as a "sinful nation, people weighed down with iniquity" (Isaiah 1:4) and warned that God would close his eyes when they prayed, because "your hands are covered with blood"! (verse 15). They rebuked great kings—"You are the man!" (2 Samuel 12:7)—and even fellow prophets—"Woe to the shepherds who are destroying and scattering the sheep of My pasture!" (Jeremiah 23:1). The Gospels model full disclosure, too. Tucker Malarkey tells us the early Christians pretended the disciples were "sinless" and "infallible," but in the space of two paragraphs, without noticing that she contradicts herself, she sarcastically notes, "Even his own church admits to Peter's irresolute character.... This is the rock on which our church is built."[2]

Truth is the rock on which the Christian church is built. The Gospels tell the truth about the holy apostles because all truth is God's truth. More importantly, they tell us the truth about Jesus.

The Gospels drive us to the "living center" of biblical tradition, Jesus Christ. As warped as any mind, age, or civilization may grow, if we hold to that center, he will push us toward life.

But one needs a touch of humility to find truth. We must not cut and paste the facts we like to fit our personal philosophy. The key is to let Jesus rebuke my philosophy, along with my sin.

There is a more humble form of identity theft that the New Testament teaches us to practice. "Take My yoke upon you," said Jesus (Matthew 11:29). "I am in My Father, and you in Me, and I in you" (John 14:20). "If anyone is in Christ, he is a new creature," said Paul (2 Corinthians 5:17).

It is worthwhile to study the great identity thieves of the past—saints, teachers, missionaries. None got it quite right. They knew that. It is also worth getting to know, and learning from, those in our families, churches, and neighborhoods who hint at the stolen character of Christ. The Gospels, which tell the truth about Jesus, are the place to begin that welcome act of burglary. They offer an easy and impossible target. The door is open wide, but like the hoard guarded by the dragon Smaug, the treasures inside take more than a lifetime to haul off, and a new adventure comes with each pilfering.

# NOTES

## Chapter 1—The Gnostic Renaissance

1. Dan Brown, *The Da Vinci Code* (New York: Doubleday, 2003), p. 248.

2. Ibid., p. 231.

3. Bart Ehrman, *Lost Christianities: The Battle for Scripture and the Faiths We Never Knew* (New York: Oxford University Press, 2003), p. 6.

4. Marvin Meyer, *The Gospel of Thomas: The Hidden Sayings of Jesus* (New York: HarperSanFrancisco, 1992), p. 111.

## Chapter 2—What Is Gnosticism?

1. Arthur Nock, cited in Elaine Pagels, *The Gnostic Gospels* (New York: Vintage Books, 1981), Introduction.

2. C.S. Lewis, *The Last Battle* (New York: Macmillan, 1956), p. 161.

3. John Sieber, *Nag Hammadi Library: The Definitive Translation of the Gnostic Scriptures Complete in One Volume,* James Robinson, ed. (Leiden, the Netherlands: E.J. Brill, 1978).

4. Accessed at www.snant.com/fp/archives/gnosticism-and-nature/.

5. Karen King, *The Gospel of Mary of Magdala* (Santa Rosa, CA: Polebridge Press, 2003), p. 44.

## Chapter 3—Gnosticism Rebooted

1. C.S. Lewis, *The Last Battle* (New York: Macmillan, 1956), p. 70.

2. Mircea Eliade, *Myth and Reality* (New York: Harper & Row, 1963), pp. 5-6.

3. Elaine Pagels, *The Gnostic Gospels* (New York: Vintage Books, 1981), p. xxxiii.

4. *The Lost Gospel: The Quest for the Gospel of Judas Iscariot* (Washington, DC: National Geographic, 2006), p. 183.

5. Pagels, *The Gnostic Gospels*, p. 153.

6. See, for examples, Paul Vitz, *Psychology as Religion: The Cult of Self-Worship* (Grand Rapids: Eerdmans, 1977), and Earnest Becker, *The Denial of Death* (New York: Macmillan, 1975). The latter, which won a Pulitzer Prize, describes how astonished Becker, an atheist, was to find how great psychological minds agreed with Christian theology about our need for God.

7. Pagels, *The Gnostic Gospels*, p. 7.

8. Ibid., p. 9.

9. Tucker Malarkey, *Resurrection* (New York: Riverhead Books, 2006) p. 329.

10. Pagels, *The Gnostic Gospels*, p. 12.

11. Will Durant, *Caesar and Christ: A History of Roman Civilization and of Christianity from Their Beginnings to A.D. 325* (New York: Simon & Schuster, 1944) p. 652.

12. Michel Foucault, *Power—Essential Works, 1954-84, vol. 3* (New York: New Press, 2001), p. 161.

13. Pagels, *The Gnostic Gospels*, p. 61.

14. Ibid., p. 70.

15. Bart Ehrman, *Lost Christianities: The Battles for Scripture and the Faiths We Never Knew* (New York: Oxford University Press, 2003), p. 4.

16. Pagels, *The Gnostic Gospels*, Introduction.

17. James Robinson, *The Secrets of Judas: The Story of the Misunderstood Disciple and His Lost Gospel* (New York: HarperSanFrancisco, 2006), p. 173.

18. Note, for example, the increasingly peevish tone of his interactions with the philosopher William Lane Craig as found at http://www.holycross.edu/departments/crec/website/resurrdebate.htm.

19. "The Judas Gospel: Decoding the Secrets of a 1,700-Year-Old Text," *National Geographic*, May 2006, p. 91.

20. Ibid.

21. Ibid.

22. Ibid.

23. "Behind the Da Vinci Code: The Mystery of Mary Magdalene, *Newsweek* (May 29, 2006), p. 47.

24. Ibid.

25. Marvin Meyer and Esther A. De Boer, *The Gospels of Mary, The Secret Tradition of Mary Magdalene, the Companion of Jesus* (New York: HarperSanFrancisco, 2006), p. 96.

## Chapter 4—There Are No Gnostic Gospels

1. Madeleine L'Engle, *A Circle of Quiet* (New York: HarperSanFrancisco, 1972), p. 24.

2. *Random House Webster's College Dictionary* (New York: Random House, 1999), s.v. "gospel."

3. *Merriam Webster's Collegiate Dictionary* (Springfield, MA: Merriam Webster's, Inc., 2003), s.v. "gospel."

4. Elaine Pagels, *The Gnostic Gospels* (New York: Vintage Books, 1981), p. 159.

5. G.K. Chesterton "The Strangest Story in the World," *Everlasting Man*, (Ft. Collins, CO: Ignatius Press, 1993).

6. Matthew 12:24.

7. Lin Yutang, *Xinyang zhi Lu* (Hong Kong: Tao Sheng Publishing, 1999), p. 246.

8. I assume, I think, with the majority of scholars, that *Thomas* borrowed from about every layer of the biblical Gospels, as John Meier showed in *A Marginal Jew: Rethinking the Historical Jesus* (New York: Doubleday, 1991), p. 137.

9. Robert Funk, *Honest to Jesus* (New York: HarperSanFrancisco, 1996), p. 161.

10. Ibid., p. 202.

11. N.T. Wright, *Jesus and the Victory of God* (Minneapolis: Augsburg Fortress Press, 1996), p. 189.

12. A transcript can be found on Wikipedia at http://en.wikipedia.org/wiki/Senator,_you_are_no_Jack_Kennedy.

## Chapter 5—"Gnostic Christianity" Is a Contradiction in Terms

1. Bart Ehrman, *Lost Christianities: The Battles for Scripture and the Faiths We Never Knew* (New York: Oxford University Press, 2003), p. 6.

2. James Robinson, *Trajectories Through Early Christianity* (Philadelphia: Fortress Press, 1971), p. 270.

3. Richard Hays, *First Things,* October 1994, correspondence.

4. N.T. Wright, *Jesus and the Victory of God* (Minneapolis: Fortress Press, 1996), p. 180.

5. Karen King, *The Gospel of Mary of Magdala* (Santa Rosa, CA: Polebridge Press, 2003), p. 39.

6. Elaine Pagels, *The Gnostic Gospels* (New York: Vintage Books, 1981), p. 152.

7. See Glenn Miller's thorough response at http://www.christian-thinktank.com/stil13.html.

8. Edwin Yamauchi, *Pre-Christian Gnosticism* (Grand Rapids: Eerdmans, 1973), p. 184.

9. See Tarif Khalidi, *The Muslim Jesus: Sayings and Stories in Islamic Literature* (Cambridge: Harvard University Press, 2001).

10. A point the influential sociologist of religion, Rodney Stark, has made for decades.

11. See David Marshall, *True Son of Heaven: How Jesus Fulfills the Chinese Culture* (Seattle: Kuai Mu Press, 2002).

12. Pagels, *The Gnostic Gospels,* p. 108.

13. John Crossan, *Jesus: A Revolutionary Biography* (New York: HarperSanFransisco, 1994), p. 66.

## Chapter 6—Nothing the Gnostics Say Happened, Did

1. Elaine Pagels, *The Gnostic Gospels* (New York: Vintage Books, 1981), p. 70.

2. Mahatma K. Gandhi, *Autobiography: The Story of My Experiments with Truth:* (New York: Dover, 1983).

3. Tarif Khalidi, *The Muslim Jesus; Sayings and Stories in Islamic Literature* (Cambridge: Harvard University Press, 2001), p. 69.

4. All *Judas* quotes are from *National Geographic* Web site.

5. Robert W. Funk, *The Five Gospels* (New York: Macmillan, 1993).

6. David Marshall, *Why the Jesus Seminar Can't Find Jesus, and Grandma Marshall Could: A Populist Defense of the Gospels* (Seattle: Kuai Mu Press, 2004).

7. Funk, *The Five Gospels,* pp. 523-4.

8. The same objections apply to *Thomas* saying 31, which Helmut Koester (in *Trajectories Through Early Christianity*) singles out as most likely to predate

the Gospel version: "Jesus said, 'No prophet is accepted in his own village; no physician heals those who know him.'" The saying about the prophet is also quoted in all four Gospels. The physician saying is unique to *Thomas*, but in Luke, Jesus says, "No doubt you will quote me that proverb, 'Doctor, cure yourself,' and you'll tell me, 'Do here in your hometown what we've heard you've done in Capernaum.'" Obviously, the Luke account makes sense; the *Thomas* account does not. Doctors often do treat people they know; they do not usually treat themselves. Jesus' teachings made sense. The same cannot, unfortunately, be said about *Thomas*.

9. Karen King, *The Gospel of Mary of Magdala* (Santa Rosa, CA: Polebridge Press, 2003), p. 110.

10. "The Judas Gospel: Decoding the Secrets of a 1,700-Year-Old Text," *National Geographic*, May 2006.

## Chapter 7—The Gospels Tell the Truth About Jesus

1. Robert Funk, *Honest to Jesus* (New York: HarperSanFrancisco, 1996), p. 179.

2. A.N. Wilson, *Jesus, a Life* (New York: W.W. Norton, 1992), p. 155.

3. Mahatma K. Gandhi, *Autobiography: The Story of My Experiment with Truth* (New York: Dover, 1983), pp. 243-4.

4. Tal Brooke, *Avatar of Night* (Berkeley: End Run Publishing, 1999), p. 56.

5. Karen King, *The Gospel of Mary Magdala* (Santa Rosa, CA: Polebridge Press, 2003), p. 84.

6. Ibid., pp. 87-88.

7. Marvin Meyer and Esther A. De Boer, *The Gospels of Mary* (New York: HarperSanFrancisco, 2006), p. vii.

8. Elaine Pagels, *Beyond Belief, The Secret Gospel of Thomas* (New York: Random House, 2003).

9. Tucker Malarkey, *Resurrection* (New York: Riverhead Books, 2006), p. 247.

10. M. Scott Peck, *In Search of Stones* (New York: Hyperion, 1995), p. 394.

11. N.T. Wright, *Jesus and the Victory of God* (Minneapolis: Fortress Press, 1996), p. 132.

12. Ibid., pp. 129-30.

13. "The Judas Gospel: Decoding the Secrets of a 1,700-Year-Old Text," *National Geographic*, May 2006, p. 91.

14. Robert Funk, *The Five Gospels* (New York: HarperSanFrancisco, 1997), p. 145.

15. Michael Wilkins, *Jesus Under Fire: Modern Scholarship Reinvents the Historical Jesus*, see chapter 5 (Grand Rapids: Zondervan, 1995).

## Chapter 8—Jesus Was the "Original Feminist"

1. Margaret Mead, *Coming of Age in Samoa* (New York: Morrow Quill Paperbacks, 1961).

2. Dan Brown, *The Da Vinci Code* (New York: Doubleday, 2003), p. 125.

3. Elaine Pagels, *The Gnostic Gospels* (New York: Vintage Books, 1981), p.71.

4. Tucker Malarkey, *Resurrection* (New York: Riverhead Books, 2006), p. 308.

5. Walter Wink, *Engaging the Powers* (Minneapolis: Augsburg Fortress Press, 1992), p. 129.

6. Rene Girard, *I See Satan Fall Like Lightning* (New York: Orbis, 2001).

7. Marvin Meyer, *The Gospel of Thomas: The Hidden Sayings of Jesus* (New York: Harper San Francisco, 1992), p.111.

8. Marvin Meyer and Esther A. De Boer, *The Gospels of Mary* (New York: HarperSanFrancisco, 2006), p. 84.

## Chapter 9—The Gospel Brings True Sexual Liberation

1. John R. Miller, at a lecture at Discovery Institute in Seattle in 2006.

2. Yasmeen Mohiuddin, *Country Rankings by the Status of Women Index,* The 1996 Conference of the International Association for Feminist Economics, June 21-23, 1996; accessed at http://by106fd.bay106.hotmail.msn.com/cgi-bin/getmsg?msg=A76AF79F-BEBB-4E.

3. Rodney Stark, *The Rise of Christianity* (New York: HarperSanFrancisco, 1997), p. 99.

4. For every 1000 boys in the Hindu community, there were only 925 girls; in the Christian community, 994. Prakash Louis, *The Emerging Hindutva Force: The Ascent of Hindu Nationalism* (Indian Social Institute, 2000), p. 182. In some wealthy regions, the ratio of girls has dropped much lower recently. Drs. Paul and Margaret Brand explained to me that Christian families often set aside "dowry" money for "extra" girls to give them a medical education: Thus many nurses in India are Christians from the state of Kerala.

5. Stark, *The Rise of Christianity,* p. 109.

6. Marvin Meyer and Esther A. De Boer, *The Gospels of Mary* (New York: HarperSanFrancisco, 2006), p. 83.

7. Rebecca Overmyer Velazquez, *Christian Morality Revealed in New Spain*, volume 10, number 2.

8. Gu Weiming, *Jidujiao yu Jindai Zhongguo Shehui* (Shanghai, China: People's Publishing Co., 1996), p. 315 (my translation).

9. Ibid., p. 313.

10. Shakuntala Narasimhan, as quoted by Ruth Mangalwadi, *The Legacy of William Carey* (Wheaton, IL: Crossway Books, 1993), p. 31.

11. Ibid., p. 36.

## Chapter 10—Gnosticism Would Not Set the World Free

1. Elaine Pagels, *Beyond Belief: The Secret Gospel of Thomas* (New York: Random House, 2003), p. 57.

2. If one substitutes *archon* for *meme,* much that Richard Dawkins and Daniel Dennett have written about religion is almost Gnostic. A *meme* is a "cultural unit of transference," a habit, song, or (more to the point) religious dogma. Dennett's *memes* almost have a mind of their own. They work "unobtrusively." They "conceal their true nature" from human hosts. They "acquire tricks," "exploit" romance, "proliferate," and "benefit" from adaptation. "Once allegiance is captured" by these bodysnatchers, "a host is turned into a rational servant," though the initial capture is usually not "a rational choice by the host." It is remarkable how durable animistic habits of thought can be. Daniel Dennett: *Breaking the Spell: Religion as a Natural Phenomena* (New York: Viking, 2006).

3. Steve Emmel, as quoted by James Robinson, *The Secrets of Judas* (New York: HarperSanFrancisco, 2006), p. 175.

4. Marvin Meyer, *The Gospel of Thomas: The Hidden Sayings of Jesus* (New York: HarperSanFrancisco, 1992), p. 111.

5. Ibid., pp. 111-12.

6. Burton Mack, *The Lost Gospel: The Book of Q and Christian Origins* (New York: HarperSanFrancisco, 1994).

7. Meyer, *The Gospel of Thomas,* pp.111-12.

8. Vishal Mangalwadi, *Truth and Social Reform* (London: Hodder & Stoughton, 1989), p. 68.

9. Hans Joachim Klimkeit, *Gnosis on the Silk Road: Gnostic Texts from Central Asia* (New York: HarperSanFrancisco, 1993), p. 20.

10. Rodney Stark, *The Victory of Reason* (New York: Random, 2005), pp. 61-62.

11. Ibid.

## Chapter 11—Jesus Brings True Freedom

1. On a flight to London last year I watched Al Gore's *An Inconvenient Truth*, a documentary about global warming. On a return flight, I flew over the magnificent ice fields and glaciers of southern Greenland. Despite Al Gore, Greenland is not in imminent danger of sloughing off into the Atlantic ocean.

2. David Aikman tells the story in detail in a dissertation, most unfortunately not published, *The Role of Atheism in the Marxist Tradition, 1979.*

3. C.S. Lewis, *Perelandra* (New York: Macmillan, 1944).

4. Donald Treadgold, *Freedom: A History* (New York: New York University Press, 1990), p. 32.

5. Vincent Carroll and David Shiflett, *Christianity on Trial* (San Francisco: Encounter Books, 2002), p. 26.

6. Rodney Stark, *For the Glory of God* (Princeton: Princeton University Press, 2003), pp. 290-365.

7. Alan Burgess, *The Inn of the Sixth Happiness* (New York: Bantam, 1971), p. 39.

8. John Farquhar, *Modern Religious Movements in India* (New York: Macmillan, 1915), p. 433.

9. Ibid., p. 441.

## Chapter 12—Meniggesstroeth Didn't Make Your Mind

1. Richard Dawkins, *The Selfish Gene* (New York: Oxford Press, 1976), p. 198.

2. Alister McGrath, *Dawkin's God: Genes, Memes, and the Meaning of Life* (Malden, MA: Blackwell Publishing, 2005), p. 84.

3. Stephen Jay Gould's, *Nonoverlapping Magisteria,* available at www.stephen jaygould.org/library/gould_nomahtml.

4. As cited at www.vatican.va/holy_father/john_paul_ii/encyclicals/documents.

5. Elaine Pagels, *The Gnostic Gospels* (New York: Vintage Books, 1981), p. 5.

6. Dan Brown, *The Da Vinci Code* (New York: Doubleday, 2003), p. 149.

7. Tucker Malarkey, *Resurrection* (New York: Riverhead Books, 2006), p. 337.

8. Pope John Paul II, *Fides et Ratio, Encyclical Letter of the Supreme Pontiff John Paul II to the Bishops of the Catholic Church on the Relationship Between Faith and Reason, 1998.*

9. McGrath, *Dawkins' God,* p. 198.

10. James Conner, *Kepler's Witch* (New York: HarperSanFrancisco, 2004), p. 91.

11. McGrath, *Dawkins' God.*

12. Ibid.

13. C.S. Lewis, *Obstinacy of Belief, in The World's Last Night and Other Essays* (New York: Harcourt Brace, 1960).

14. N.T. Wright, *The Resurrection of the Son of God* (Minneapolis: Augsburg Fortress Press, 2003), p. 718.

15. Ibid., p. 372.

16. Rodney Stark, *For the Glory of God* (Princeton: Princeton University Press, 2003), pp. 121-99.

17. Carola Baumgardt, *Johannes Kepler: Life and Letters* (New York: Philosophical Library, 1951), p. 31.

18. Brian Greene, *The Elegant Universe* (New York: W.W. Norton, 1999), p. 387.

## Chapter 13—Spinning Jesus

1. Mary Brian Durkin, "Dorothy Sayers: A Christian Humanist for Today" (*Chistian Century*, November 14, 1979), p. 114.

2. Tucker Malarkey, *Resurrection* (New York: Riverhead Books, 2006), p. 247.